To:

From:

Date:

Heart

of the Holidays

Holiday Inspirations
Yuletide Treasures & Traditions

Sheryl L. Roush

Sparkle Press
San Diego, California

Published by Sparkle Press
A division of Sparkle Presentations
Post Office Box 2373, La Mesa, California 91943 USA

Send contributions to Sheryl@SparklePresentations.com

Visit our website at: www.SparklePresentations.com

First Printing September 2007

Library of Congress Control Number: 200790324

ISBN: 978-1-88087-815-6

Library of Congress Cataloging-in-Publication Data
Roush, Sheryl Lynn.
Heart of the Holidays
Holiday Inspirations
Yuletide Treasures & Traditions/Sheryl L. Roush
    ISBN 10: 1-880878-15-1
    ISBN 13: 978-1-880878-15-6
    1. Holidays 2. Inspirational 3. Self-Help

Printed in Canada.

*T*he truest "holiday," or "holy day"
is in the essence of gratitude we
carry in our heart, and live in each day. Not
a date on a calendar. Celebrating holidays
gives us an opportunity to pause from daily
to-do's and survival to find greater meaning
and significance in our life.

~ SHERYL ROUSH

Holidays Over the Years

THANKSGIVING

THEN Dad carving the hard-crusted turkey with electric knife, nibbling as he goes.

NOW Dad carving the moist, baked-in-the bag turkey, without the electric knife, still nibbling as he goes.

THEN Mom cooked up real cranberries (too lumpy for me).

NOW Sheryl brings jellied cranberry sauce with pickled beets.

THEN Never decorated the house for the fall holiday.

NOW Decorate with autumn leaves, real pumpkins, and golden garlands.

THEN Showed up in time to eat, everything was fixed by mom, departed early with leftovers in Tupperware and plastic baggies.

NOW Arrive early, set the table, bring healthy food choices to add to the menu, clear the table after the meal, and wash the fine china, stay late just to hang around and have meaningful conversations.

CHRISTMAS

THEN Snow skiing in the mountains, freezing with friends.

NOW Kaua'i Island, Hawaii at brother's garden paradise.

THEN Frantic, last minute shopping on Christmas Eve.

NOW Carefully selecting the gifts for loved ones throughout the year.

THEN Dragged guys under the mistletoe.

NOW Avoid being dragged under the mistletoe.

THEN Dipping candy canes into hot chocolate.

NOW Dipping chocolate mint candy canes into Starbucks coffee.

THEN Ungrateful for gifts; selfish and expecting.

NOW Truly cherish and appreciate whatever is given to me.

THEN Bought fresh-cut trees, not supporting the environment.

NOW Grow my own potted Norfolk pine tree that is now 8' tall.

Holidays Over the Years

THEN Tossed the tree into the dumpster after two-three weeks,
NOW Encourage neighbors to recycle their trees, instead of creating waste.

THEN Eggnog loaded with rum and sprinkled with nutmeg.
NOW Lactose-intolerant . . . sparkling apple cider.

THEN Purchasing next year's cards the day after Christmas, usually on sale.
NOW Custom, thinking of each recipient, starting as early as October.

THEN Gave angels and candles for holiday gifts.
NOW Receiving angels and candles as gifts—throughout the year.

THEN Hated reading stupid letters people sent with their cards.
NOW Look forward to reading those wonderful letters from loved ones.

THEN Tossed those stupid letters people sent with their cards.
NOW Joyfully write a thoughtful letter to send out with my own cards.

THEN Ate a *lot* of chocolate.
NOW *Give* more chocolate and sweets than I eat.

NEW YEAR'S EVE

THEN Making resolution lists easily broken in the first week.
NOW Writing out manifestation goals for the entire year.

THEN Partying all night long, waking up with hang-overs.
NOW Meditation and vision boarding, and off to bed early.

THEN Looking back with disappointment over what I hadn't done.
NOW Celebrating with deep gratitude of accomplishments, adventures, joys throughout the year.

NEW YEAR'S DAY

THEN Getting up early to watch the Rose Parade with mom, shown once.
NOW Watching the broadcast of the parade any of the multitude times.

~ SHERYL ROUSH

Heart of the Holidays

With praise, we welcome the Holidays,
We express our love for God and man,
We celebrate each special date,
In the very best way we can.
One God . . . one world . . . for us all,
Yellow or Black or White or Brown,
Joined in spirit, mind, and heart,
Holiday Time . . . our common bond.
Thanksgiving turkeys, cranberry sauce,
Hanukkah candles, Christmas tree lights,
Ring out the Old! Ring in the New!
Heart of the Holidays . . . God's delight!

~ VIRGINIA (GINNY) ELLIS
© *July 2005*
www.poetrybyginny.com

Contents

♦ ♦ ♦

Thanksgiving

HAPPY THANKSGIVING

The turkey is cooking; we've all been to church,
Our grandparents soon will arrive.
The table is set; the best linen is used,
What a grand day to be alive!

There's a nip in the air; we're planning on snow,
We kids have new scarves and new muffs.
The cat, a new bell—the dog, a new bow,
And the phone is ringing for us.

"Hurry up, kids! Talk to great Uncle Joe,"
Who lives a long ways away.
Then we'll call Cousin Jo and dear Auntie Flo,
And wish them joy today."

Oh, something special there is in the air,
And not just good smells from the oven.
The holiday feeling is felt everywhere,
"Come on, darlin,' give Mama some huggin.'"

The kitchen door opens; the food is brought in,
We kids all race to the table.
Napkins are snugly tucked 'neath our chins,
We are hungry, willing and able.

(continued)

(CONTINUED)

Dad starts to carve, right after grace,
Then my brother shouts, "Dibs on a leg!"
Mom has a special smile on her face,
Our dog sits at Dad's knee and begs.

"Please pass the beans." "Where are the yams?"
"Does anyone want a roll?"
"That turkey is almost as big as I am."
"Who emptied the gravy bowl?"

So the feast moves on straight to the pie,
I rub my tummy; it's so full.
But I'm no piker—oh no—not I,
"Whipped cream, if you please, a big spoonful."

So, with warmth and laughter and much good cheer,
For this day, we send thanks above.
We're grateful we've all been together this year,
"Thank You, Dear Lord for such love."

~ VIRGINIA (GINNY) ELLIS
© 2001, 2003, 2004, 2007
www.poetrybyginny.com

THANKSGIVING

Gratitude is the sign of noble souls.

~ AESOP

Thankfulness is the beginning of gratitude.
Gratitude is the completion of thankfulness.
Thankfulness may consist merely of words.
Gratitude is shown in acts.

~ HENRI FREDERIC AMIEL

Gratitude unlocks the fullness of life. It turns what we have
into enough, and more.

~ MELODIE BEATTIE

Gratitude makes sense of our past, brings peace for today and
creates a vision for tomorrow.

~ MELODIE BEATTIE

Remember God's bounty in the year.
String the pearls of his favor.
Hide the dark parts, except so far as they are breaking out in light!
Give this one day to thanks, to joy, to gratitude!

~ HENRY WARD BEECHER

The unthankful heart . . . discovers no mercies; but let the thankful heart sweep through the day and, as the magnet finds the iron, so it will find, in every hour, some heavenly blessings!

~ HENRY WARD BEECHER

Sometimes we need to remind ourselves that thankfulness is indeed a virtue.

~ WILLIAM BENNETT
Author and politician

When you consciously choose to see the good that is already present in your life, you immediately open up the floodgates for more good to come your way.

~ RHONDA BRITTEN

Gratitude helps you to grow and expand; gratitude brings joy and laughter into your life and into the lives of all those around you.

~ EILEEN CADDY

It is literally true, as the thankless say, that they have nothing to be thankful for. He who sits by the fire, thankless for the fire, is just as if he had no fire. Nothing is possessed save in appreciation, of which thankfulness is the indispensable ingredient. But a thankful heart hath a continual feast.

~ W.J. CAMERON

When it comes to life the critical thing is whether you take things
for granted or take them with gratitude.
~ G.K. CHESTERTON

Gratitude is not only the greatest of virtues, but the parent
of all the others.
~ CICERO

If the only prayer you said in your whole life was, "thank you,"
that would suffice.
~ MEISTER ECKHART

For each new morning with its light,
For rest and shelter of the night,
For health and food, for love and friends,
For everything Thy goodness sends.
~ RALPH WALDO EMERSON

To speak gratitude is courteous and pleasant, to enact gratitude is
generous and noble, but to live gratitude is to touch heaven.
~ JOHANNES GAERTNER

Gratitude is the memory of the heart.
~ FRENCH PROVERB

Wake at dawn with a winged heart and give thanks for another day of loving.
~ KAHLIL GIBRAN

The hardest arithmetic to master is that which enables us to count our blessings.
~ ERIC HOFFER

I'm thankful for my eyes—that I might see spectacular sunsets, lovely flowers of spring, the sweet face of a child.

I'm thankful for my ears—that I might hear the birds' sweet songs, children's infectious laughter, glorious music that uplifts the soul.

I'm thankful for my lips—that I might help kiss away a child's tears, whisper words of love, share encouragement and praise.

I'm thankful for my hands—that I might help a neighbor in need, hold hands with loved ones, give a warm hug or pat on the back.

Most of all, I'm thankful for my mind—that holds all these memories—so that, when I feel sad or discouraged, I can once again recall all these wonderful gifts with which I've been blessed.
~ CONNIE JAMESON

Thanksgiving

As we express our gratitude, we must never forget that the highest appreciation is not to utter words, but to live by them.

~ JOHN F. KENNEDY

Let us be grateful to people who make us happy; they are the charming gardeners who make our souls blossom.

~ MARCEL PROUST

If I have enjoyed the hospitality of the Host of this universe, Who daily spreads a table in my sight, surely I cannot do less than acknowledge my dependence.

~ G.A. JOHNSTON ROSS

Giving gratitude—that spirit of thankfulness—expands our receptivity to receive, strengthens our abundance to share, and deepens our heart's desires to give even more.

~ SHERYL ROUSH

At times our own light goes out and is rekindled by a spark from another person. Each of us has cause to think with deep gratitude of those who have lighted the flame within us.

~ ALBERT SCHWEITZER

He who thanks but with the lips
Thanks but in part;
The full, the true Thanksgiving
Comes from the heart.

~ J.A. SHEDD

No matter how miserable you are feeling, take the time to be grateful. Start with, I am thankful the sun is shining today; I am thankful I am alive; I am thankful I am not a refugee in Iraq; I am thankful I am not starving today. When you start this list in your mind, you will be surprised to see how much gratitude you feel, and it will put into perspective what is really important and you will soon find that your miserable feelings are banished.

~ TERRY SWEENEY

Gratitude is our most direct line to God and the angels. If we take the time, no matter how crazy and troubled we feel, we can find something to be thankful for. The more we seek gratitude, the more reason the angels will give us for gratitude and joy to exist in our lives.

~ TERRY LYNN TAYLOR

Walk the world with gratitude.

~ ST. JOHN'S UNITED CHURCH OF CHRIST, 1957 SERMON

Gratitude makes sense of our past, brings peace for today, and creates a vision for tomorrow.

~ UNKNOWN

Gratitude is the inward feeling of kindness received. Thankfulness is the natural impulse to express that feeling. Thanksgiving is the following of that impulse.

~ HENRY VAN DYKE
American short-story writer

Feeling gratitude and not expressing it is like wrapping a present and not giving it.

~ WILLIAM ARTHUR WARD

Grace isn't a little prayer you chant before receiving a meal. It's a way to live.

~ JACKIE WINDSPEAR

The more you praise and celebrate your life, the more there is in life to celebrate.

~ OPRAH WINFREY

Be Thankful

Be thankful that you don't already have everything you desire.
If you did, what would there be to look forward to?
Be thankful when you don't know something,
for it gives you the opportunity to learn.
Be thankful for the difficult times.
During those times you grow.
Be thankful for your limitations,
because they give you opportunities for improvement.
Be thankful for each new challenge,
because it will build your strength and character.
Be thankful for your mistakes.
They will teach you valuable lessons.
Be thankful when you're tired and weary,
because it means you've made a difference.
It's easy to be thankful for the good things.
A life of rich fulfillment comes to those who
are also thankful for the setbacks.
Gratitude can turn a negative into a positive.
Find a way to be thankful for your troubles,
and they can become your blessings.

~ AUTHOR UNKNOWN

Thanksgiving, after all, is a word of action.

~ W.J. CAMERON

Thank God for this glorious day. I shall rise, rejoice, and be glad in it. Thank you for every way in which I experience your Love—through giving, sharing, and receiving. Use my life. I am your messenger.

~ SHERYL ROUSH
Speaker, author of Sparkle-Tudes! *and* Heart of A Mother, *www.SparklePresentations.com*

"Modeh Ani"
"I am grateful before you."
These are the first words you are to say in the morning in traditional Jewish life. When you start the day being grateful, the hectic morning rush (kids, dog, sandwiches, backpacks) falls into perspective . . . (if you have a moment to think about it).

~ LINDA KAPLAN SPITZ, M.D.

Families are like fudge . . . mostly sweet with a few nuts.

~ UNKNOWN

RECIPROCI–TEA

God gives and returns to me from within me.
I look out, I look in, and God is all I see.
God is all there is.
Eternal giving and eternal receiving—
together they work in complete harmony.
Like a dance choreographed so beautifully.
We flow together, live together, move, and have our being as one.
This interchange is mutual and divine and mine.
I claim it. I claim God for me and good for me.
All I sow, I shall reap—this is God's law.
Love and good manifest for me now.
To take back or take away is never God's way.
I choose my words and thoughts carefully.
I pray from a place of security.
I respect God's laws of reciprocity and generosity.
I am grateful for this rule, for the way it is.
I remember to surrender and trust what is.
I have faith in how things will come back to me.
And so they do, and so it is, and so I let it be.
Amen

~ DARLENE FAHL-BRITTIAN
Author, speaker, certified tea specialist
www.takeupthecup.com

Thanksgiving is the holiday of peace, the celebration of work and the simple life . . . a true folk-festival that speaks the poetry of the turn of the seasons, the beauty of seedtime and harvest, the ripe product of the year—and the deep, deep connection of all these things with God.

~ RAY STANNARD BAKER (DAVID GRAYSON)

Turkey: A large bird whose flesh, when eaten on certain religious anniversaries has the peculiar property of attesting piety and gratitude.

~ AMBROSE BIERCE
The Devil's Dictionary

The family. We were a strange little band of characters trudging through life sharing diseases and toothpaste, coveting one another's desserts, hiding shampoo, borrowing money, locking each other out of our rooms, inflicting pain and kissing to heal in the same instant, loving, laughing, defending, and trying to figure out the common thread that bound us all together.

~ ERMA BOMBECK

What we're really talking about is a wonderful day set aside on the fourth Thursday of November when no one diets. I mean, why else would they call it Thanksgiving?

~ ERMA BOMBECK
"No One Diets on Thanksgiving," 26 November 1981

Other things may change us, but we start and end with the family.
~ ANTHONY BRANDT

Stand up, on this Thanksgiving Day, stand upon your feet. Believe in man. Soberly and with clear eyes, believe in your own time and place. There is not, and there never has been a better time, or a better place to live in.
~ PHILLIPS BROOKS

When you look at your life, the greatest happinesses are family happinesses.
~ DR. JOYCE BROTHERS

On Thanksgiving Day we acknowledge our dependence.
~ WILLIAM JENNINGS BRYAN

For, after all, put it as we may to ourselves, we are all of us from birth to death guests at a table which we did not spread. The sun, the earth, love, friends, our very breath are parts of the banquet . . . .Shall we think of the day as a chance to come nearer to our Host, and to find out something of him who has fed us so long?
~ REBECCA HARDING DAVIS

THANKSGIVING

Thanksgiving is America's national chow-down feast, the one occasion each year when gluttony becomes a patriotic duty.

~ MICHAEL DRESSER

If you ever start feeling like you have the goofiest, craziest, most dysfunctional family in the world, all you have to do is go to a state fair. Because five minutes at the fair, you'll be going, ya know, we're alright. We are dang near royalty.

~ JEFF FOXWORTHY

Where we love is home, home that our feet may leave, but not our hearts.

~ OLIVER WENDELL HOLMES

Call it a clan, call it a network, call it a tribe, call it a family. Whatever you call it, whoever you are, you need one.

~ JANE HOWARD-FELDMAN

An optimist is a person who starts a new diet on Thanksgiving Day.

~ IRV KUPCINET

Forever on Thanksgiving Day,
The heart will find the pathway home.
~ WILBUR D. NESBIT

I have strong doubts that the first Thanksgiving even remotely
resembled the "history" I was told in second grade. But considering
that (when it comes to holidays) mainstream America's traditions tend
to be over-eating, shopping, or getting drunk, I suppose it's a miracle
that the concept of giving thanks even surfaces at all.
~ ELLEN ORLEANS

Thanksgiving Day is a jewel, to set in the hearts of honest men; but
be careful that you do not take the day, and leave out the gratitude.
~ E.P. POWELL

Not what we say about our blessings, but how we use them, is the
true measure of our thanksgiving.
~ W.T. PURKISER

Thanksgiving is an authentic holiday, without the commercialism, in
its purest form of gratitude and sharing matters of the heart, sharing
quality time with family members and cherished friends, then topping
it off with fresh homemade pumpkin pie and whipped cream.
~ SHERYL ROUSH

Thanksgiving dinners take eighteen hours to prepare.
They are consumed in twelve minutes.
Half-times take twelve minutes.
This is not coincidence.

~ ERMA BOMBECK

And though I ebb in worth, I'll flow in thanks.

~ JOHN TAYLOR

You don't choose your family.
They are God's gift to you, as you are to them.

~ ARCHBISHOP DESMOND TUTU

Thanksgiving Day, a function which originated in New England two or three centuries ago when those people recognized that they really had something to be thankful for—annually, not oftener—if they had succeeded in exterminating their neighbors, the Indians, during the previous twelve months instead of getting exterminated by their neighbors, the Indians. Thanksgiving Day became a habit, for the reason that in the course of time, as the years drifted on, it was perceived that the exterminating had ceased to be mutual and was all on the white man's side, consequently on the Lord's side; hence it was proper to thank the Lord for it and extend the usual annual compliments.

~ MARK TWAIN

SWEET AWAKENINGS

*T*hanksgiving has always been my favorite holiday. Ever since I was a child my mother held the tradition of hosting Thanksgiving. I have come to treasure this tradition when various family members and friends come together for a day of hanging out with the people I care deeply about but don't see very often throughout the year.

The preciousness of this time came through clearly during Thanksgiving 2001. My niece Hilary was almost four years old at that time. That Thanksgiving we were both once again visiting her nana (my mother). Hilary and I shared the guest room with two twin beds. Hilary awoke that morning way before my wake-up time. After a few moments of stirring about and just after I was hoping she had decided to go back asleep, she hopped out of bed and declared innocently, "Aunt Laura, time to wake up." To which I promptly replied, "No it's not" in the same sweet sing song tone and trying to stay asleep. Hilary was confused and asked, "Why?" Isn't that the most favorite three-year-old question?

I tried explaining that I was still tired and wanted to sleep, but she didn't quite get it. So instead of trying to explain any further, I suggested she bring her pillow over to my bed and rest next to me. She liked that idea. It must have sounded fun to her. So upon her resting her head on her pillow on my bed, she began speaking. She said, "Aunt Laura?" And I said hesitantly, "Yes?" with one eye open seeing two big beautiful brown eyes gazing at me. To which she replied with such sweet sincerity gazing right into my eyes, "I love you." Well isn't that the most precious way to wake up?

(continued)

SWEET AWAKENINGS (CONTINUED)

This is the moment that made my whole Thanksgiving. I am so grateful for the young people in our lives who bless us with their love unconditionally and freely.

I relive that moment over and over just to feel the rapture of being alive in any given moment. Such sweetness provides the rich essence in our lives. I believe that it's a reminder to spend moments thinking about where we can express our love and be present to others' expression of love toward us. May we all share a little more love this holiday season and remain in deep gratitude for the love that others so courageously share with us.

~ LAURA RUBINSTEIN
Speaker, professional coach, certified hypnotherapist
www.transformtoday.com

The only rock I know that stays steady, the only institution I know that works is the family.

~ LEE IACOCCA

AN OPPORTUNITY TO RECONNECT

I awoke Thanksgiving Day of 1994 terrified at the prospect of spending the day with my big brother Lee and his family. Even in the best of families holidays are often filled with stress. Thoughts of eccentric uncles, screaming siblings, and burnt food fill the air with apprehension about creating yet another less than spectacular holiday memory.

My feelings of dread were not borne on memories of the past, but on fear of the future, for this holiday would forever be known as "Our First Thanksgiving."

He left home when I was six months old. My big brother Lee and I had never shared a Thanksgiving table. I knew I had a brother; I had simply resisted the urge to go looking for him. Like most foster kids, I had passed through lots of doors, many of which I slammed shut. As I boarded the morning flight from Florida to California, I wondered what kind of memories we would create on that special day.

The journey actually started months earlier when I received Lee's first e-mail, which I almost deleted because of the unfamiliar address. As I automatically moved to press delete, the subject line caught my eye, "Looking for my lost brother." I sat there for quite some time, not sure if I wanted to open a big door to a painful past.

I almost didn't, but Jenny was in the hospital. A little voice told me something important was about to happen. I replied to Lee's message and told him I was going to Maine to be with his niece who, although she struggled to control her diabetes, had just graduated from high school.

I put thoughts of my brother aside as I spent Sunday with Jenny in the hospital as the staff rehydrated her and reduced her blood sugar to a safe level. We were all relieved when they moved her from ICU to a regular room.

(continued)

AN OPPORTUNITY TO RECONNECT (CONTINUED)

I don't have the words to describe the emotions that flooded in when I got the call at eleven that night that Jenny was gone. The next week of meetings with doctors and funeral directors, and the funeral itself were mostly a blur, but I remember the quiet phone calls with my big brother, who gave me hope. These thoughts were on my mind during the flight to California: "What kind of strange dishes would be on the table?" and "What if my brother was an ax murderer?"

At Lee's house I was greeted by my family, their neighbors, and *ABC News*. It was a struggle to get out of the car, and Lee had to be dragged down the driveway by his wife Dorothy.

There was nothing to fear. We shared a great feast and exchanged presents. Lee presented me with a watch, and the news camera captured my emotion as I read the inscription on the back, "For the time we've lost. Love, Lee."

Our first Thanksgiving was immensely stressful, but incredibly memorable. We had an even bigger event on our tenth anniversary. On Thanksgiving Day 2004 our other brother Earl T. chose to celebrate with us. Once again we had a great feast. This time it was my turn to present watches to my brothers, but with a slightly different inscription that read, "Thanks for the times we've had. Love, Jerry."

As you prepare to celebrate your family's special events this holiday season, let me leave you with the thoughts I expressed in a news interview that first Thanksgiving, "As we approach the holidays, I hope everyone who hears our story will use it as an opportunity to reconnect with their family." May this holiday season give you and your family the best of times and create many happy memories.

~ JERRY GITCHEL
Excerpted from "Me, Lee, and Earl T., The Bond of Brothers," http://gitchel.com/thebondofbrothers

WHAT MATTERS MOST

*T*he room Grampa relaxes in after a long day of hard, physical labor has been transformed—just for today. All of our family will soon gather in this used-to-be-bedroom in the small apartment where Mom and Auntie Sharon grew up after their relocation from a small Minnesota town.

My sister, Kellene, and I wear festive, crisply pressed aprons that Nana keeps especially for us. The perfectly fanned bows are tied to anchor the gauzy fabric around us as it flows from our waists— just like Nana's "dress-up" apron does. Committed to our kitchen responsibilities, we still find time here and there to play with our brother, John, and our cousins.

In the living room, pipe tobacco glows red in Grampa's left hand, as his right rests on the arm of his easy chair. The wonderful fragrance of it rests gently on the air and fills my lungs with each breath. Dad and Uncle Keith are exchanging stories and reminiscing about who ate "the most" tacos during our family's summer gatherings.

Wherever I am in the small apartment, I see smiling faces and hear laughter! Every room is alive with nurturing aromas of wholesome food, prepared precisely and exactly as it has been through many, many years gone by.

Intently, I watch the preparations occur before my very eyes, and I revel in the once-again timeless repetition of these family traditions tenderly handed down from my greats and great-greats. What is done, how is it accomplished, and by whom? Mom, Auntie Sharon, and Nana work together like orchestra musicians playing the finest of concertos. Kellene and I model their lead as we train for our future as beneficiaries of the family traditions.

(continued)

WHAT MATTERS MOST (CONTINUED)

After days of anticipation and preparation, it's finally time to enjoy our meal together. The long church table has been hauled in from Grampa's woodworking studio a stone's throw from Nana's kitchen view under the canopy of the towering avocado tree, and past the porch swing where Nana lacquer-paints our little girl nails. It fills the center of yesterday's bedroom with barely enough space for our bodies to occupy the chairs around it.

We gather excitedly to give thanks and celebrate all that is good. Nana's best dishes and silverware adorn the table. Tall, frosty glasses of water and Auntie Sharon's vibrant napkins decorate every place setting. Serving dishes of steaming entrees, colorful side dishes, and traditional Thanksgiving temptations occupy the remaining table space. The centerpiece is a limited edition, one-of-a-kind, "designer original" work of art. And it's not really in the "center" of the table, but more toward one side. My side, luckily.

On the edge of a chair tucked between tall, adult bodies I love dearly, my ten-year-old eyes observe our centerpiece with delight and amazement. Our new infant cousin, Keisha, wearing the tiniest of lace-trimmed stockings and a holiday-print jumper, reclines safely atop the table in her infant seat. She watches the activity around her with alert, liquid-brown eyes; and, takes in the sounds with pearl drop ears Mom often soothes with "Raindrops are Fallin' on My Head." Her fair hands and feet move with excitement.

I look around and my heart overflows as I feel how blessed my family is through the birth and recent adoption of this so-wanted child! It is November 1971 and this new life—and those that exist now and others that will follow later—are what matters most.

~ BELINDA SANDERS
Freelance writer and business coach, www.belindasanders.com

THANKSGIVING 365 DAYS A YEAR

*H*ave you noticed that we appreciate things more when we lose them? I know I did before being diagnosed with multiple sclerosis at the age of twenty-three in 1986. I went from a competitive athlete to being paralyzed from the neck down. Since that time, I have experienced numerous attacks of paralysis and blindness with varying degrees of recovery in between.

Now, I give thanks each night for the senses that I *do* have, rather than the abilities I have lost. It's amazing how beautiful a sunset is when you've lost your eyesight for a few weeks or how enjoyable a walk along the beach can be when you've been confined to a wheelchair, paralyzed for nearly a month. Since regaining my ability to walk, I truly appreciate playing a round of golf with my husband and traveling internationally. Years ago when I was in a wheelchair during Canadian Thanksgiving, I decided to go to a medical healing retreat in Baja California, Mexico. My recovery was so terrific that I was able to enjoy a "personal best" golf round one month later during Thanksgiving weekend. I savored that turkey dinner in more ways than one! During times when I have lost my sense of touch and feeling to the degree that I could no longer appreciate the softness of my pet's fur, I would take action with an "attitude of gratitude" and book an appointment at a spa—when my legs were numb, it was an ideal time to have them waxed!

Of all the holidays I celebrate each year, I enjoy Thanksgiving the most because it's an opportunity to share with my loved ones the lessons I have learned about never taking things for granted and especially, to treat *every* day like it's Thanksgiving Day. I encourage them to practice Jack Canfield's quote: "Each night when you go to sleep, try counting your blessings, instead of just counting sheep."

~ JAN MILLS
Speaker, health and wellness coach, www.janmills.net

A DIFFERENT THANKSGIVING

For many years our family has gathered at Aunt Jan's house in Huntington Beach for Thanksgiving. Aunts, uncles, cousins, and friends come to share news, enjoy each others' company and partake in the wonderful feast of food. Several of us live in Southern California and make it a point to attend while some cousins come from as far away as Hawaii, Alaska, and Washington State. We play games, bounce babies on knees, and sing along with Cousins John and Bob who bring their musical instruments to entertain us. It's a great time to reminisce and catch up on each others' lives. It's not often those of us who live in the area miss a Palmer Thanksgiving.

One year I saw an ad in the newspaper for a four-day-trip to Acapulco with a price I couldn't believe! Having never been there before I thought, *wow, what a fun weekend*. I called up the travel agency hosting the trip and found it was over Thanksgiving weekend. What to do? How could I miss our annual feast? (Despite the fact that I hate turkey!) Then it came to me, my birthday was the Friday after Thanksgiving. Why shouldn't I treat myself for my birthday? Yes, I would miss the family terribly but . . . it was something different to do for my birthday and that holiday weekend.

I flew with a small group to Acapulco the Wednesday before Thanksgiving. We arrived to sunshine and clear skies while back in California it was clouding up. On Thanksgiving, while the major hotels were having a buffet of turkey, several of us went to Carlos and Charlie's for fish tacos and Margaritas. We toasted our families back in the states and marveled at the fresh air, sunshine, and good food!

When I returned from that idyllic weekend, I found that they had experienced a torrential rain storm on Thanksgiving Day. That was one time I was thankful I decided to have a different Thanksgiving.

~ BECKY PALMER

THE LAST PIECE OF PIE

It was I.
I cannot lie.
It was I,
Who ate the last piece of pie.
It lay there in the fridge.
I thought I would eat just a midge.
But, oh it tasted so good,
and put me in such a happy mood.
Each bite made another bite.
I really did try to fight,
The yearning for just a bit.
Oh, mother is going to have a fit,
For the pie is all gone.
But, I cannot tell a lie.
It was the most scrumptious pie,
And all I wanted was just a bit.
But once begun I could not cease.
Now the last piece,
Will bring me no peace,
For I had finished the pie.

~ LILLIAN BERMAN

GIBLETS AND GRATITUDE

*T*hanksgiving started way before Thursday when I was growing up. The meal was served at Grandma's house. It wasn't over the river and through the woods—just over the hill. We went there lots of times, but Thanksgiving was Grandma's special treat for the family.

She made all the pies and there were *sooooo* many of them, at least a half dozen. She made them from scratch with a little help from Libby's for the canned pumpkin, into which she stirred the eggs, milk, and spices including pungent ginger, cloves, and plenty of cinnamon. I was astounded at how she could get that flour, shortening, and water to turn out as a delicious flaky crust. I became even more amazed as I grew older and tried to do it myself with much less spectacular results and great deal of flour all over the floor.

More memories come from remembering Wednesday evening, the eve of Thanksgiving. That was when the "good" girls got to go help with the next set of preparations. Not everyone could fit in her tiny kitchen, so we vied for the privilege. The bread was torn into small pieces and allowed to dry in the gigantic dishpan over night. The onions and celery were diced and set aside for the morning when they would be mixed with the bread, butter, and another set of fragrant spices like sage, thyme, pepper, and poultry seasonings. How did we know it was right? Grandma knew, just by the taste! To this day, I don't measure any of the ingredients, I just know, from the taste.

The turkey, all twenty-five pounds of it, was cleaned in the kitchen sink after removing the enclosed "innards." It always slipped and slid around as if it was still alive. The "innards" cooked with onions and celery made the best giblet gravy! The turkey sat overnight, in the fridge, in its dishtowel blanket, until the preparation of the stuffing was completed in the morning.

(continued)

GIBLETS AND GRATITUDE (CONTINUED)

Then the task of stuffing all that dressing into the bird became top priority. We stuffed the center cavity and then the neck and sewed it all together using thread on a big needle. It took a big pan to hold that bird but Grandma had just the one and she placed it in the oven covered with an aluminum foil "tent" to allow it to become a gorgeous, golden brown. What a heavenly aroma reached our noses as we came through her kitchen door for dinner that evening.

The table was also set the night before with her fancy dishes that I never saw any other day of the year. To this day, I remember the dove gray color with the white flower in the center and the shiny silver trim of her china. Wiped clean of dust, all the place settings included four dishes and five pieces of silver placed just so on the holiday napkins. Oh, it was elegant!

But that is not where I sat. That was the table for adults! The kids table was set up the next day in the living room. There we lined up place settings of harvest colored paper plates for each kid.

Over the years, these celebrations grew to serve eight adults and fifteen children. Eventually all of those fifteen kids grew up, moved all over the United States, created their own families and started their own traditions.

One year after I moved to California, with a failed relationship weighing down my heart, I faced the holiday without family, far away and on my own. My new neighbor and landlady became a great friend. We planned my second Thanksgiving in California together. The menu included all the traditional fare and her added Italian delicacies. Her side of the duplex was the venue. Her whole family, Grandma and Uncle Freddy, her godmother, her brother with his wife and child, were invited. I invited my cousin Jerry.

(continued)

GIBLETS AND GRATITUDE (CONTINUED)

I am an obstetrician and was on call that Thanksgiving. Obviously, I was taking chances that I could do my part for the celebration. Then, oops! A baby's birthday took precedence and I never made it to dinner at all! Thank goodness, my cousin is as gregarious as he is. He had Thanksgiving with a whole group of people he had never met. They welcomed him warmly, fed him extravagantly, and sent him on his way with the requisite "doggy bag." I received my share of the leftovers when I got home.

Maybe that was a sign of things to come. Thanksgiving is the holiday I host each year. I always seem to have one or more persons, who I have never met, come for dinner. One year, my friends brought their neighbors and the neighbor's sister who was visiting from Canada. My little friends were ballet dancers and as *The Nutcracker* was always in rehearsal in late November, several dancers from other countries were guests one year. I have had guests and their friends from my church.

All are welcome. There is always plenty. I can't seem to learn how to roast less than twenty pounds of turkey. That still seems to be just the right size, despite the smaller crowd at my house. Maybe the cooking lessons, "stuffed" into me by my mother as she cooked for the twelve members of our family every day, are too ingrained to be undone. She would have died of embarrassment if there were not enough food when feeding guests. Everyone needed to be full to overflowing!

As the years go by, I like to recall what that full feeling means. Full tummy, full heart, the atmosphere full of love, joy, and prosperity. When we come together, share our human souls, and join in showing how much we appreciate each other and everything we have been given, it feels like a slice of heaven.

(continued)

GIBLETS AND GRATITUDE (CONTINUED)

A quote from the author and minister Max Lucado sums it up for me. *Gratitude: More aware of what you have than what you don't.* I need that reminder to stop and be grateful for everything, because I know how wonderful my life is. I have my health, good friends, work that I love, family who are there for me. I have more things than an individual needs.

I have had my share of manageable challenges that did not look quite so manageable when I was in the midst of living through them. I wanted to be a doctor for as long as I can remember. We had no doctors in my family. We had no money to fund all that education. I worked and paid my own way through college and medical school.

I am grateful for the few who believed in me, who knew I could, even when I thought I couldn't. Mr. Peterman, my pharmacist boss, for whom I worked during high school as a clerk and soda jerk, believed in me. Judy Shoaf, my Girl Scout leader, turned friend to this day, believed wholeheartedly. I had to learn to be grateful for those who didn't believe in me. My resolve to show them that I could do it became the angry fire in my gut, which powered me through the tough times, when I may have quit the course.

Finding the many things for which to be grateful is easy when you practice. I taught my little friend Lara to review at the end of the day what we called "happy thoughts" and this was our form of thanksgiving. I taught my dad in his late seventies to look for a positive in every day, even if it only consisted of the fact that the lights went on when he flipped the switch. He was able to feel the beauty in life toward the end of what had been a long trail of poverty, health challenges, and early loss of his wife.

(continued)

GIBLETS AND GRATITUDE (CONTINUED)

And, for myself, I now remember each night to stop and thank the universe for yet another spectacular day, whatever its form. My expanded point of view helps me realize that thanks can be given not only on one day or one week, but all 365 days a year.

~ CAROL GRABOWSKI
Speaker, contributing author to Heart of a Woman *and* Heart of a Mother

OUR DAILY BREAD

When my daughters were growing up we always bought wheat bread. Sandwiches, toast, French toast, you name it, it was wheat bread. When the girls were about three and five, we bought white flour dinner rolls for our Thanksgiving dinner. Our guests were seated at the table, the turkey was being carved, and I cut a roll in slices for the girls. I'm not sure what she thought we'd been eating all along, but when I put a slice on her plate, my three-year-old said, "Oh! Clean bread!"

~ JOAN ENGUITA
www.joanenguita.com

GRANDMA'S CORNBREAD

*B*efore my grandmother passed away, I asked her to teach me to make her cornbread. Her cornbread wasn't a regular store-bought concoction or pre-measured ingredients that you bake for so much time. When Grandma made cornbread, she did it by feeling. Her measuring spoons were her hands and fingers, and the texture of the batter told her all she needed to know. When Grandma cooked, the whole neighborhood showed up, and they were always welcome.

Ever since her death, I had been apprehensive about trying to make her cornbread. Out of all the extended family members, not one of the myriad children, grandchildren, cousins or in-laws had her recipe. That teaching lesson years ago was my only guide, and I was terrified that I could never remember enough to make it worth the time to try.

For Thanksgiving one year, my husband and I invited our families to come to our new house. Everyone was excited; this would be the first holiday dinner we had all celebrated together in a long time. When my mother asked me to make cornbread dressing, I agreed. The week of Thanksgiving arrived, and I remembered the cornbread I would need to make to fulfill my mother's request. With trepidation bordering on blind faith, I tried to recall that lesson taught long ago.

As I began measuring and mixing ingredients, it was as if Grandma was there beside me, guiding me. I could hear her words in my ear, "No, dear, you're going to need more cornmeal than that . . . don't forget to use buttermilk . . . pinch of sugar . . . ." My measuring cups forgotten, I plunged my hands into the cold, gritty cacophony of textures and began weaving it into a symphony of resplendent remembrance.

Time fell away, and I was suddenly young and baking with my grandmother again. I poured the entirety of my creation into the awaiting skillet, and thrust it into the oven with a prayer.

(continued)

GRANDMA'S CORNBREAD (CONTINUED)

As I cleaned the kitchen, Sunday school songs and trips to Grandma's house flooded my memories. For the first time in years, I remembered my grandmother; the way she made everyone welcome at her table and in her home; the way she cared for my grandfather until his dying day, and the way she cared for everyone else until her own; her assurance that she would always be watching over us, right by her Lord's side, until our times came to see her again. As the afternoon wore on, I began to swear I could smell the aromas of my grandmother's kitchen, there in my own house. Then I remembered my cornbread.

I opened the oven with the fear of a child on her first day of school. Mommy, will the other children like me? Will I like them? Will the teacher be nice? Will I make you proud? With feelings of eternity stretching out in that one moment, I removed the skillet from the oven with a soft gasp. There, rising over and above the skillet's rim, was my grandma's cornbread. Gingerly, I lifted it out; into my awaiting hand, I flipped the full pan of cornbread, a solid mass of golden, glistening sunshine, and turned it over onto the cooling rack. In shock, I called my mother in tears. "I made Grandma's cornbread! And it's beautiful!" I told her. I took pictures with my phone and sent them to her, too excited to convey the intimacy of these new feelings within my soul.

At Thanksgiving dinner, as we shared our memories of Grandma, my six-year-old son asked me where she was. "Grandma is in heaven, honey," I explained. After a pause, and with the look of childhood innocence, he asked me, "Mommy, when you're in heaven, will you come back to help me make cornbread, too?" The truth of his young wisdom touched us all as we agreed that, indeed, Grandma had been there with us on that Thanksgiving Day.

~ JENNIFER M. PLOSSL
www.jpcreative.photoreflect.com

Christmas

For God so loved the world, that he gave his only begotten Son, that whosoever believeth in him should not perish, but have everlasting life.

~ JOHN 3:16

May the spirit of Christmas bring you peace,
The gladness of Christmas give you hope,
The warmth of Christmas grant you love.

~ ANONYMOUS

Christmas gift suggestions:
To your enemy, forgiveness.
To an opponent, tolerance.
To a friend, your heart.
To a customer, service.
To all, charity.
To every child, a good example.
To yourself, respect.

~ OREN ARNOLD

Christmas is love, it's in the songs we're singing
Christmas is love, it's families comin' home
Christmas is love, it's on the children's faces
Christmas is love
We all gather 'round, watch the lights dancing on the tree
The spirit of the season, you feel it in the air
Christmas is love.

~ WORDS BY ALABAMA
Volume II Christmas CD, Song lyrics by Rich Alves, T.J. Knight, and Jerry Taylor

THE GIFT OF LOVE

One year my mama knitted me a scarf and sweater as a holiday gift. They were soft and white and reminded me of a kitten. Friends at school showed off their expensive gifts but . . . the things my friends had couldn't compare to the homemade treasures that my mama had made for me. I learned an important lesson that year. It was that things don't matter, but that people who love you do, and the things they create are the most important gifts of all. I wear that scarf and sweater to this day knowing Mama's love is with me.

~ SELENA PARKER

Blow, blow, Bethlehem wind, over the hills and the valleys.
Blow, blow, Bethlehem wind, God's promise of love and salvation,
Blow, blow, Spirit of Truth, carry the news of a Saviour.
Blow, blow, Spirit of God, preparing the world for God's Son.
Blow, blow, Spirit of Hope, scatter the leaves of our sorrow.
Blow, blow, Spirit of God, warm the whole world with your love.
Alleluia.

~ SONG LYRICS BY JOSEPH M. MARTIN

We all get so hung up on material things at times
It seems like we forget what Christmas really means
It should be thanks we're givin', that's why I wrote this tune
Happy birthday, Jesus, this song is just for you

~ WORDS BY ALABAMA
Song lyrics by J.P. Pennington and Teddy Gentry

THE GREATEST STORY EVER TOLD

Do you remember?
Have you ever known
Of that night in December
When the brightest star shown?
Have you heard the story told
Of that fateful night of old?
The Virgin Mary, the unborn baby,
Looking for a place to stay.
"There is no room in the inn,"
They heard time and time again;
One had compassion, an older fashion,
And led them to the stables.
A newborn babe laid his head,
With a manger for a bed;
The star twinkled bright, with eternal light,
On the baby laid in hay.
Shining angels came to talk;
To shepherds that watched their flock
"I have tidings great," angels did dictate,
"And news of great joy tonight."

~ REBECCA BRINCK

Love is, above all, the gift of oneself.
~ JEAN ANOUILH

I am not alone at all, I thought. I was never alone at all. And that, of course, is the message of Christmas. We are never alone. Not when the night is darkest, the wind coldest, the world seemingly most indifferent. For this is still the time God chooses.
~ TAYLOR CALDWELL

I wish we could put some of the Christmas spirit in jars and open a jar of it every month.
~ HARLAN MILLER

And she gave birth to her firstborn son and wrapped him in swaddling cloths and laid him in a manger, because there was no place for them in the inn.
~ LUKE 2:7

Celebrate the happiness that friends are always giving,
Make every day a holiday and celebrate just living!
~ AMANDA BRADLEY
Poet, author

THE LORD'S BIRTHDAY PARTY
So many candles on His cake,
Their lights were seen on earth,
It was heaven's grandest party,
Held in honor of His birth.

A birthday party for the Lord,
Oh, such excitement up above,
The angels planned for days on end,
To shower Him with gifts of love.

They prepared a festive banquet,
And baked an angel cake,
And every soul in heaven
Was invited to partake.

The banquet hall was filled with flowers,
Their scent like sweet perfume,
And graceful, crystal chandeliers
Cast dancing lights about the room.

The dining tables were adorned
With fine cloths of handmade lace,
Along with gleaming silverware,
And sparkling china set in place.

(continued)

(CONTINUED)

Every resident of heaven
Was requested to attend,
Though long ago on earth below,
They had been invited then.

All guests were dressed their very best,
In snow-white robes with golden trim,
They wore broad smiles of joy
As, arm-in-arm, they entered in.

To get the party started,
Gabriel blew his holy horn,
Then angels sang sweet songs of praise,
Announcing Christ was born.

More than two thousand years before,
God had sent His son to earth,
And now these souls were here because
Of that precious baby's birth.

Oh, what a gala gathering!
What good cause to celebrate!
The birth of Jesus Christ on earth!
The most wonderful of dates!

(continued)

(CONTINUED)

Parties, too, were held on earth,
But nothing quite like this,
Though folks below could look above.
And see His candles lit.

Each twinkling star, a flickering flame
Of a candle on His cake,
A trillion, tiny lights above,
To scintillate and fascinate.

Let earth and heaven celebrate!
Let the bells ring out galore!
A Merry Christmas to us all!
And a Happy Birthday to our Lord!

~ VIRGINIA (GINNY) ELLIS
© December 2005
www.poetrybyginny.com

WHAT COLOR IS YOUR JESUS?

My husband-to-be had a bleak view of church when we first met. His overriding memory of Sunday school was being punished at age three for coloring Jesus purple.

What the teacher saw as disrespect was more likely a foreshadow of Mark's artistic talent. Do you think Jesus minded being purple? I don't. Every culture depicts Jesus a little differently. I have seen fair-skinned, blue-eyed Jesuses (or is it Jesi?), black ones, Asian ones, and in my friend Ellen's nativity scenes from Mexico, a beautiful brown-eyed, toasty-skinned baby Jesus.

In reality, Jesus probably sported a swarthy complexion, with dark eyes and black hair, like many of the Middle Easterners we see today. But what is more important than color is size. There is no doubt Jesus was an infant. So, next time you see a child, think about Jesus, and how much he loved us to become a baby that burped and spit up. Think about how he might have said his first words or taken his first step.

The color of Jesus' skin doesn't matter because if he lives in our hearts, he does look just like we do.

By the way, Mark still isn't exactly wild about Sunday school, but he likes purple. Best of all, he loves Jesus!

~ LORRI V. ALLEN
Speaker, author, www.lorri.com

A TIME
Yuletide
A time of Celebration,
Bringing closure to the old year,
Setting resolutions for a better life,
Making goals for the next year.

A time of Gratitude,
Expressing to those near and dear to us,
A special fondness in our hearts.

A time of Hope,
Hope for a better future,
Hope for deeper meaning on our lives,
Hope for strengthened family ties.

A time of Forgiveness,
Letting by-gones be truly by-gone,
Starting anew with fresh, clean slates.

A time of Love,
Expressed candidly,
Sharing more openly our true feelings to others.

A time of Peace,
A deep longing for harmony,
Reunion, collaboration, trust.

A time of Spirit.
Celebrating our soul's profound wisdom of the ages,
Rekindling our uniqueness and collectiveness
as we are *one* on the planet,
We are the Family of God.

(continued)

(CONTINUED)

A time of Reconnection,
Being back in touch with those we've not seen or heard from in ages,
and picking back up the conversation right where we left off.

A time of Hearts,
Bonding for the first time,
Reuniting from separation,
Deepening in trust,
Pure, innocent, Divinely connected,
Connection so deep, it's beyond words.

A time of Humor,
Laughing over advertises won.
Telling our tales of tribulations,
Seeing the irony of it all.
Sharing stories of our life's adventures,
Recognizing our common journeys.

A time of Love,
Knowing that we are truly loved,
Not for what we have, or for presents given, or promises made,
Just because.

Unconditional, non-judgmental,
The love that connects us all—one heart to the other,
Our Divine umbilical cord soul to soul,
Heart to heart.

~ SHERYL ROUSH
Speaker, author, www.sparklepresentations.com

KITTY'S CHRISTMAS PARTY

'Twas the night before Christmas, and all through the house,
Not a creature was stirring, except for the cat.

The stockings were shredded, by the chimney with care,
For Kitty had decided to express her artistic flair.

The children were bundled warmly in bed,
While thoughts of wild mayhem ran through Kitty's head.

Ma and Pa wearily went to bed and turned out the lights,
Leaving Kitty alone in the house for one wild night.

Through the house she stole, stalking all the shadows,
She shredded the ribbons and battered all the bows.

She attacked the presents, the paper she ripped and tore,
And left the remains scattered all over the floor.

The Christmas tree stood all alone and still,
Upon it Kitty pounced, intent on making the kill.

Something went wrong, the tree stood its ground,
Kitty thought fast, other amusement was still to be found.

She looked at the ornaments, aglow in the dim light,
And batted them all with feline delight.

Soon an ornament broke free and crashed to the floor,
Kitty watched it shatter, and then sent down some more.

(continued)

(CONTINUED)

As the night wore on, Kitty got bored with the tree,
She climbed down and surveyed her victory.

The house was a disaster, everything was all over the floor,
But Kitty soon found that to this she could still add more.

She attacked the ruined stockings with renewed glee,
And added unraveled yarn to the remains under the tree.

Kitty soon realized that she was ready for a snack,
She drank Santa's milk, nibbled a cookie, and then launched the rest
in another attack.

She batted the cookies all through the house,
All the while being quite as a mouse.

She found small presents and scattered them across the floor,
The house was a disaster from door-to-door.

Kitty wreaked havoc all through the remainder of the night,
She found she was getting tired as dark gave way to light.

In the morning the family surveyed the house with despair,
And found dear Kitty soundly asleep in a chair.

~ MICHELLE WEISSER
© *December 1992*

KEEPING IT RUSTY

There was no snow, which was not unusual for a January evening in Canada, but the cold had definitely come to stay. I could see my breath. And, it was cold enough to be physically felt on my cheeks as I returned home from work. At that moment, all I wanted to do was to get inside my home, warm up with a strong cup of tea, and think about what I was going to make for dinner. I had a long day with the responsibilities of a full time job and being a mother. The last thing I wanted to think about or deal with was someone else's problems.

Someone else's problems became mine quickly, however, as I heard a meow come from around the corner of my house. Investigating the source of the noise, I discovered a three-month-old orange colored kitten huddling in a bare bush beside the house. He approached me immediately, looking for help. As I picked him up, he started purring, his shivering body cuddling into mine as he searched for warmth.

Before long, he was a family member in a house with two other cats who did not always appreciate his unique personality.

Rusty quickly discovered that both cats could easily be approached from behind, pounced on, and left far behind as he quickly attacked and dashed out of reach. He took great pleasure in taunting these two older maiden aunts who were unable to do much to stop him. They would hiss at him and make the occasional swipe in his direction, but because he was much younger, leaner, and faster, he easily ran circles around them. They did, however, receive daily satisfaction at Rusty's expense. It was easy to see that they enjoyed watching Rusty get into trouble as he knocked over a plant or ripped up a newspaper. Watching him from a comfortable distance, they frequently looked as if they were thinking, "What an idiot."

(continued)

KEEPING IT RUSTY (CONTINUED)

Watching that little orange nuisance, I discovered that some cats are just born odd. No matter how often he got squirted with water or I shook a can of pennies at him, he never seemed to learn. Rusty seemed to embody the philosophy, "It is better to seek forgiveness then ask permission."

Through the spring and into the summer, Rusty, now an indoor cat, found new and inventive ways to get into trouble. He also managed to rid our house of three mice at Thanksgiving.

If it's possible for a cat to have Attention Deficit Hyperactive Disorder, I think Rusty owns and embraces it. Any slight movement or flicker of light would attract his attention. Once he was after the new source of interest, he would climb over furniture and people to get to it. So it shouldn't have been a surprise when he managed to escape on Christmas day. With all the excitement in the house and the coming and going of family and friends, Rusty somehow found a way outside. As we searched for him, first inside, and then outside of the house, I'd swear that both of my other cats were smiling. When he didn't return that night, I became worried.

Later on the following day, I learned that sweet little Rusty had himself quite a night. He was staying at the local animal shelter. I found out when I phoned the shelter on the off chance he might be there. When I dropped by to pick up the wayward ball of fluff, I was told Rusty's story from some very glad-to-see-me shelter staff.

A neighbor, who was fed-up with a feral cat getting into his garbage, had set up a cat trap. Rusty's bold fearlessness did not serve him well that day. He became trapped in the cage and was taken to the animal shelter. Rusty's first victim was a young woman who made the mistake of attempting to handle him on her own.

(continued)

KEEPING IT RUSTY (CONTINUED)

He easily escaped her and knocked over a stack of empty animal travel carriers as he headed into the next room—full of stray dogs. Luckily for Rusty, the much larger animals were in cages. However, the din must have been incredible for the poor staff and for Rusty when, suddenly, a streak of orange flashed by with nowhere to go but up. He bounced over the cages until he found a corner, and quickly backed into it. The staff person retreated until she could find back-up.

The two young women approached Rusty for a second time. They were met with teeth, claws, and a noise that could only be described as the sound of tortured souls in hell. Quickly backing away, the two young women only gave Rusty yet another path to escape. He bolted back into the room where the cats were lodged, jumping on a desk of paper files that poured onto the floor. Then, he was up and into the window, wedging himself between the two panes of glass. Rusty was eventually caged, and continued to complain vigorously until I arrived. As I paid the $40 fee to have him returned to me, the two young women told me about the adventures of Rusty. None of it was a surprise to me. I knew what he was like.

As I picked him up and cuddled him, preparing to take him home, his little body began to shiver, reminding me of the first day that I had found him. He was an older cat now, but he still made it plain that he needed me. I brought him home. As his feet touched the carpet and he knew where he was, he relaxed and behaved as if he had never left, walking away to look for the other two cats so he could torment them some more. His homecoming was not quite the Christmas gift everyone expected. Everyone was glad to see him, of course, except my two other cats who had become used to having their home back. I am sure that they each gave me a dirty look for bringing him.

(continued)

KEEPING IT RUSTY (CONTINUED)

I later discovered a rough patch of skin on Rusty's nose. The veterinarian informed me that Rusty had ringworm. Rusty had gone out for a night on the town. He had gotten himself arrested and thrown in jail. He also had instigated a prison riot and attempted an escape. I bailed him out and brought him home, receiving not one sign of thanks, and to top it off, he had brought home a communicable disease.

Despite the consequences, Rusty has demonstrated that he knows how to have a good time. As I watch him discover new ways to amuse himself by chewing on a box, shredding a carpet, or pulling down a blind to get to a window, I remember the first day I found him and brought him into the house. He doesn't realize it, but he has given me a Christmas gift. Rusty has taught me that there is more to life than being responsible all the time and always doing what is right. We are also meant to have a little fun.

~ PATRICIA STEWART

TEN ROBINS AND A PINE TREE

*A*n icy cold wind blew as hard as it could, tossing ten small robin red breasts through the sky as if they were dry leaves. As strong as they were and as well as they could fly, they were blown off their course and became lost.

They were dropped into a forest, but didn't realize where they were because they had always lived in woodlands, swamps, parks and gardens. The north wind blew even harder, tossing the birds among tall trees with spindly, leafless limbs. When the snow began to fall and land on their wings, they became frightened. There were no leafy trees where they could cuddle and keep warm.

Exhausted, one robin landed on a bare limb that grew on a tree's far side. At least the tree trunk blocked some of the icy wind. The other nine birds followed him and all lined up, sitting as close as they could to each other. The tree's limb shook and trembled. "Get off of my limb," the tree grumbled. "You are tickling me and it's irritating."

"Can't we rest just for a moment?" asked one of the birds. "We are lost and cold. We only need to rest a minute."

"Rest somewhere else," said the tree. "I don't want you in my limbs." The small birds fluffed their feathers, trying to capture all the warmth they could from each other, then one by one, they flew off.

Snow flakes fell at an alarming rate now, and the clouds above covered the sky and sun and made it seem like night. The tiny birds' feathers were heavy with snow. Drops of water began to freeze on their beaks' tips. They were afraid, but they bravely flew, looking for a place to land and huddle.

(continued)

TEN ROBINS AND A PINE TREE (CONTINUED)

The smallest of the tiny birds finally cried out, "I can't fly any farther." His voice was raspy and weak. The other birds knew they had to stop soon.

The ten birds alighted on a snow-covered branch of another leafless tree. The tree's branches whipped around in the wind and snow. "You birds are all cold and wet," the tree complained. "Get off my branch."

"Can't we rest here just for a while? We are tired, cold and hungry. Your trunk protects us from the wind. Please let us stay until we are warm and the sun comes out."

"I can't take care of ten birds," grumbled the huge tree. "I have to take care of myself so I have the energy to grow my new buds in the spring. Fly away now. Don't bother me."

The tiniest bird landed on the ground. "I can't fly any more. You'll have to go without me," he said. (Were the drops of water sliding down his cheeks from melting snow or were they tears?)

"We won't leave you," said one of the other birds. "We'll find somewhere to stay until we are warm and rested."

All the birds hopped around in the snow, hoping they would find somewhere to stay for a while.

"You can stay in my branches, if you want."

"Was that a voice I heard?" asked one of the birds. "Did the rest of you hear that?"

"I heard something," answered the smallest bird.

"Over here," said a tiny voice. The birds noticed the branches of a small pine tree moving. It wasn't the wind that moved the branches, because this tree was so small, it sat underneath the trunks of the tall trees. The stout trunks protected the little pine whether the big trees liked it or not.

(continued)

TEN ROBINS AND A PINE TREE (CONTINUED)

"I am close enough to the shrubs so you can reach the berries. They are very small, but they will keep you fed for a while, maybe even until spring. And my limbs are covered with needles all winter long. You will be warm and protected from the cold and snow."

The little birds couldn't believe their luck. Each bird flew up into the tree's branches, thanking the little pine with their song.

"I'm so happy to have your company," said the little pine. "It's almost Christmas and I was so sad when I thought I'd be all alone."

The robins had been so worried about finding a place to stay for the winter, they had forgotten what time of the year it was. "It is almost Christmas," said the robins. "And we have much to be grateful for thanks to you, little pine tree."

The next day was Christmas Eve. The birds had eaten a few berries and snuggled among the pine tree's branches. They awoke rested and fed. During the day the robins collected more berries and stored them throughout the little pine tree's branches. Snowflakes fell, causing the pine needles to shine and twinkle. Then the robins sat among the snowflakes and berries, puffing out their red chests. The clouds cleared as the sun went down. Stars began to twinkle in the dark blue sky. A big, bright star appeared just above the little pine tree. Its light filtered through the bare branches of the big trees, causing light to shine on the glittering snow and berries and on the robins' red breasts.

The big trees couldn't help but admire the one bright spot in the forest. They were even jealous, but instead of being grumpy, they were delighted by the sight of the bright little tree, covered in berries, sparkling snowflakes and the ten robin red breasts. The huge trees leaned in, toward the tiny pine, not only to capture some of the warmth and see the tree, but to help shelter it and the birds from the cold.

(continued)

TEN ROBINS AND A PINE TREE (CONTINUED)

Years have passed since that Christmas and now the pine tree is tall, straight and lush with green needles. He has younger pines growing under him now. Any time birds get lost and need a place to stay warm and dry until winter passes, the forest's big trees—now much kinder and more patient—lead the lost birds to the pine tree, a place where the Christmas spirit is alive all year 'round.

~ MARILYN DALRYMPLE

It came upon a midnight clear
That glorious song of old
God's child was born to earth so began
The greatest story ever told.
Wise men came to see him there
Laying in soft manger's hay
Radiant angelic hosts proclaimed
"Unto you a child is born" they say.
Centuries from that first nativity scene
From Christ's birth, we've come to hear
Of God's plan, Virgin Mary's gift
Come closer to love, and farther from fear.
Still today, we celebrate that glorious night
Midnight clear, and stars so bright
That all will know of Divine love
And great gifts from Heaven above.

~ SHERYL ROUSH
Speaker, author, www.sparklepresentations.com

Great little one! Whose all-embracing birth
Lifts earth to heaven, stoops heaven to earth.

~ RICHARD CRASHAW

For every time your own heart lightens up, there is a
positive effect in the world and you can see the light in others.

~ LISA DELMAN
Author of Dear Mom *and* Letters from the Heart Project, *www.theheartproject.com*

Life, love, and laughter—what priceless gifts to give our children.

~ PHYLLIS DRYDEN

And you shall love the Lord your God with all your [mind and] heart
and with your entire being and with all your might.

~ DEUTERONOMY 6:5

What the world needs now is love, sweet love
It's the only thing that there's just too little of.
What the world needs now is love, sweet love,
No not just for some but for everyone.

~ JACKIE DESHANNON

AND THIS IS CHRISTMAS MORN

My Cat suffers from temporary insanity . . .
gallops furiously through the house
tail hooked.
His feet make tiny explosion noises
as they hit the linoleum
above the hollow basement.
He comes to a halt
at my sleeping dog's face—
rises up:
he's a grizzly!!
Pummels the air
around sleeping Henry's nose with open cat toes—
lethally prepared.
Finds
no response
and so
saunters huffily away—
glares
at me as I laugh.
I know
he's been sitting below the baby grand piano,
the lighted Christmas tree

(continued)

(CONTINUED)

blinking from above,
reflected in the polished mahogany lid,
I can tell he's been snorting through
the ribboned presents there,
looking for his.
He hasn't waited for the family to arise,
but went ahead and found his present—
inhaled through ribboned paper,
and now
as the rest of the family still sleeps,
knowing ribboned gifts will wait—
a grizzly
prowls the magic morn.
It shoots me a look
which says:
Items sniffed through curled
red ribbons may appear larger.
Catnip powered family pet
licks his paw
and waits.

~ RETA L. TAYLOR
© 2007 Reta Lorraine Bowen Taylor

CHRISTMAS HERE ALL YEAR

We have Christmas each December,
Which is appropriate and fine,
The whole world comes together,
For Christmas at that time.

Everyone sings Christmas carols,
And pays homage to the Lord,
And if a child's good all year,
Santa brings him just rewards.

Since everyone's so happy,
And there's so much love and cheer,
Don't you think it would be grand,
To have Christmas here all year?

We could play our Yuletide music,
Whenever we desired,
And hear those songs of Christmas
That encourage and inspire.

On New Year's Eve we'd drink a toast,
Of festive, sparkling wine,
And ring out joyous Christmas bells,
While singing "Auld Lang Syne."

(continued)

(CONTINUED)

We'd hug and kiss on Valentine's Day,
(Love is such a worthy cause),
Then we'd giggle and we'd sing,
"We Saw Mommy Kissing Santa Claus."

We'd sing, "Away in the Manger,"
No crib for a bed."
While spring robins are building
Snug nests for wee heads.

"Jingle Bells, Jingle Bells,
Jingle all the Way."
Now, wouldn't that be fun to sing,
Each Saint Paddy's Day?

"Deck the Halls with Boughs of Holly,"
Cherry blossoms bloom in May,
"'Tis the Season to be jolly,"
See the hummingbirds at play.

"Joy to the World" in August,
Would make us smile and make us glad,
It would be our neighbors' problem,
If they heard our song and thought us mad.

(continued)

(CONTINUED)

When a harvest moon hangs in the sky,
And the whole world's bathed in gold,
We would think about "A Midnight Clear,"
And that glorious story of old.

I love the Christmas music,
Playing softly in my ear,
September or November,
I don't care the time of year.

Why not celebrate the Lord,
And play His music all year round,
And fill our spirits and our hearts,
With joyful Christmas sounds?

But even more than that, perhaps,
We might bring pleasure to our Lord,
By singing songs for Him all year,
"Oh, Come Let us Adore Him."

~ VIRGINIA (GINNY) ELLIS
© *March 2005*
www.poetrybyginny.com

FES-TI-VI—TEA

There is so much to celebrate.
Every moment in God is an eternity of joy.
Every moment with God is an infinity of delight.
I let go of time and rejoice in the now.
In the power of this moment, God shows me how.
I am one with the source of this jubilation,
the provider of this soul celebration.
One with divine revelry is all we really can be.
I exult in my own goodness and my own worthiness.
I have been given an invitation to celebrate all the time.
I claim back the gifts that once were mine.
With jubilee, I thank God for the wonders and joys of our divine unity.
Every day is a special occasion and a reason for celebration.
Every breath a pleasure, an ecstasy, an inspiration of divinity.
I have nothing to plan or prepare, I surrender to the Divine Host, who
is always there. The party is for me, and these gifts I share—
my light, my love, my laughter.
I know the truth of happily ever after. Thank you.
Amen

~ DARLENE FAHL-BRITTIAN
Author, speaker, certified tea specialist
www.takeupthecup.com

A CHRISTMAS POEM FOR MOM

For all the nights you stayed up late
to trim the Christmas tree,
For all the costly presents
That you purchased just for me.
For all the times you tucked me in
And read me stories too,
For all the ways you cheered me up
When I was feeling blue.
For all the cookies that you baked
And stockings that you stuffed,
For all the messes you cleaned up
and pillows that you fluffed.
For all the days you loved me,
Even when I made it difficult,
For all these things, and much, much more . . .
Merry Christmas!

~ UNKNOWN

CHRISTMAS MUSIC

*L*ooking at me, you'd probably think that holiday traditions would not be high on my priority list. I'm the designer with the funky glasses in the museum, at the jazz club, or taking road trips to New York City. Yet, when singers on store speakers remind me that *Santa Claus Is Coming to Town* my thoughts turn to holidays past. I miss the warmth and joy of being surrounded by my family; however, these days we are spread across many states. I used to spend the holidays desperately missing the old times and wishing everyone was nearby to cheer me up. But when I wake up to the blessings around me, I realize the many opportunities to spark that Christmas spirit once again, no matter where I am or who I'm with. After all, John Denver and the Muppets tell me it's time to *Deck the Halls*.

In New England, with friends, I shop for presents at local craft fairs and attend the hilarious Boston Improv holiday comedy show. I buy tea on Newbury Street, and drink it while listening to my *Christmas with the Rat Pack* holiday jazz CD with my purring cat on my lap.

At work we take a break and decorate our cubicles with lights. We switch from coffee to hot chocolate and indulge in the abundance of sweets baked by coworkers. We share our holiday albums through our iTunes libraries on our computers, especially our favorite: *Christmas Time is Here* from *A Charlie Brown Christmas*.

Then I'm off to Florida. On Christmas Day my parents and I drive to the ocean and dip our feet into the water. Later, we enjoy Mom's homemade cooking, which she generously makes vegetarian for me. The Christmas tree twinkles with family ornaments collected though the years, as we listen to the Carpenters' *O Holy Night*.

Every place can have its share of fun and moments of connection. I have realized that, indeed, *I've Got My Love To Keep Me Warm*.

~ COLLEEN CUNNINGHAM
Graphic designer, artist

INFINI-TEA PRAYER

So great are the gifts of God that they cannot be measured.

Absolute, boundless perfection is the God I know, and I know that
God is all there is.

The Force is infinite. There is no space between God and me—
we are one.

This Oneness is immeasurable and immutable. Infinite love is given
to me free of any conditions, free of any limits, and free of all
boundaries.

I am good enough to accept and embody God's love just as I am.

A love for eternity from Divine Infinity, is the greatest treasure of all.

For this gift, I feel from the core of my being a love and appreciation
beyond words.

God knows the home of love and gratitude,

this place that defies borders and

this place where words do not exist.

This is the birthplace of infinity.

From here, from within, I release all limits, all fears,

all smallness and I trust this Infinite Wisdom.

It guides me always, guards me always, and governs me all ways

For all of my days.

Amen

~ DARLENE FAHL-BRITTIAN
Author, speaker, certified tea specialist
www.takeupthecup.com

CHRISTMAS

Whatever else be lost among the years,
Let us keep Christmas still a shining thing;
Whatever doubts assail us, or what fears,
Let us hold close one day, remembering
It's poignant meaning for the hearts of men.
Let us get back our childlike faith again.
~ GRACE NOLL CROWELL

The joy of brightening a child's heart creates the magic of Christmas.
~ W.C. JONES

Little children look right through that which we have learned to be
and into the beauty of our soul. This is truly love.
~ CATHERINE TILLEY
www.theglobalvoice.com

The spiritual meaning of love is measured by what it can do.
Love is meant to heal. Love is meant to renew.
Love is meant to bring us closer to God.
~ UNKNOWN

Love is the intuitive knowledge of our hearts.
~ MARIANNE WILLIAMSON
Speaker, author of A Woman's Worth

"FAMILY CIRCUS" CHRISTMAS
Mommy Throws A Tantrum!

When I started this vocation called Mother I had it all down. I just knew my children (two, maybe three) would be the most perfect in the neighborhood. I was going to give June Cleaver a run for her money! Donna Reed . . . Ha! Betty Crocker, *oh pleazzzze*! Over and over again in my head I said Ha! Then I actually had a child. And another. And another. And another. And another . . . boy, this wasn't how I played it all out in my head! Five babies in six years! Wow! Just getting out of the house I had to find shoes to go with 50 little toes . . . oh, and the socks needed for those same 50 little piggies! It was and still is an adventure!

Christmas was a fun time at our house but a frustrating time for me personally. I could not figure out why I could not have the sit-down dinner with everyone pressed, styled, combed, clean, smiling, happy and oh so grateful, singing "Silent Night" in perfect pitch just before the "Norman Rockwell" Christmas dinner was served!

One particular Christmas I was so frustrated. I tried all the "right" things and, when that failed, I resorted to bribery, blame, lavish promises and, finally, at wit's end . . . a tantrum. Not just whine, shed a tear, then go-about-life tantrum . . . a full blown on-my-face-tantrum in the living room in front of the Christmas tree kicking my feet, pounding my fist, screaming . . . "Why?! Why? and then to have my oldest (who was all of 5 years old), come tell me "Z, Mommy. 'Z' comes after 'Y.' Don't be sad, we will work on your alphabet together! You can get it!"

Thank God he didn't know the real reason for my tantrum! I dried my tears and looked at them. Really looked at them. They were happy, perplexed at mommy at that moment, but they had all their little hearts needed. A mommy and daddy who loved them.

(continued)

"FAMILY CIRCUS" CHRISTMAS (continued)

A safe place to put their blankie and to them, a fun place to be. They had more live-in playmates than anyone they knew!

I suddenly realized what the problem was. Not the kids—not my husband—but me! Not the me me—but the attitude me.

I missed out of the real wonders of the first few Christmases because of my terrible choice of holiday comfort friends. Yep, the trio Shoulda, Coulda and Woulda and their cousins Only and If had come to once again to the Hall house to "celebrate" the year! I don't remember consciously inviting five more to our already full house . . . but nonetheless they showed up every year and seemed to be staying longer and longer! Uninvited . . . how rude!

No wonder I was so frustrated! I kept striving for the "Norman Rockwell" Christmas and kept getting "Family Circus" instead! I had my holiday comfort friends cheering me on, again. That year I gave them the boot! And I discovered "Family Circus" isn't so bad!

The Friends still try to visit occasionally, usually when my spirits are a bit down . . . but there is no room! I still hold on to the fantasy of "Norman Rockwell" Christmas dinner but only in my dreams. As I watch my pieces of Heaven laugh, run, play with each other . . . I really have made best friends with the "Family Circus." And I learned the whole alphabet too!

~ TERRI L. HALL
Contributor's request: Please do not use any part of this out of context.

Editor's note: In our conversation receiving permission to print this original work for the first time, Terri added: "In time God blessed me with a new life (in more ways than one) and now am remarried (for almost 10 years) and have a total of 12 children and 6 grandchildren with one on the way (only 7 kids are still at home). It has been an adventure!

Blessed is the season which engages the
whole world in a conspiracy of love.
~ HAMILTON WRIGHT MABIE

Peace on earth will come to stay,
When we live Christmas every day.
~ HELEN STEINER RICE

God's answers are wiser than our prayers.
~ UNKNOWN

May you continue to acknowledge,
Embrace, and radiate what can not be:
bought or sold,
never goes on sale,
maintains your health,
grows your prosperity,
creates more world peace,
keeps our home planet clean
requires no money or batteries,
magnetically attracts loving people to you,
and educates and inspires others to personal excellence
. . . your loving magnificence!
~ MARIANNE WILLIAMSON
Speaker, author of A Return to Love

BEING

Come inside and play
Close the door and come in,
Discover the wonders,
Claim them as yours!
Let life fill you,
Delight your heart,
Hear the laughter,
Feel the joy!
Walk amid the flowers,
See through the fog,
Watch the sun come up,
And play with her rays.
Catch the moonbeams,
Pull them into you,
And dance in their light,
With abandon, unfettered and free!
Soar to the heights of you,
Feel the rich soil,
Plant seeds with roots of great breadth and depth,
Harvest wisdom, love, joy, peace, and POETRY!
Coming out now,
Living from within,
Drawing on the riches,
Of my internal fertile garden!

~ KATHY HOLDAWAY
www.leadingedgeopportunities.com
© 2006 Kathy Holdaway

For the eyes of the Lord are on the righteous and his ears are attentive to their prayer.

~ 1 PETER 3:12
Women's Devotional Bible 2, New International Version

Love is the face of God.

~ AMMA (MOTHER), MATA AMRITANANDAMAYI, INDIA
Messages from Amma: In the Language of the Heart, *www.amma.org*

I find it interesting that the meanest life, the poorest existence, is attributed to God's will, but as human beings become more affluent, as their living standard and style begin to ascend the material scale, God descends the scale of responsibility at a commensurate speed.

~ MAYA ANGELOU
American poet, writer, and actress

It is this belief in a power larger than myself and other than myself which allows me to venture into the unknown and even the unknowable.

~ MAYA ANGELOU
American poet, writer, and actress

People see God every day, they just don't recognize him.

~ PEARL BAILEY

Never be afraid to trust an unknown future to a known God.
~ CORRIE TEN BOOM

When I stand before God at the end of my life, I would hope that I would now have a single bit of talent left, and could say, "I used everything you gave me."
~ ERMA BOMBECK

Some of God's greatest gifts are unanswered prayers.
~ GARTH BROOKS
Singer, song lyrics

Every evening I turn my worries over to God.
He's going to be up all night anyway.
~ MARY C. CROWLEY

There are three answers to prayers: Yes, no, and wait.
~ EMILY B. DESHAZO

It's the moment you think you can't that you realize you can.
~ CELINE DION

Seeking God is more than having a casual interest in him. It's similar to going on a hunt, and the place for us to start is God's word, where he reveals himself to us.

~ ELLEN BANKS ELWELL

God grant you the light of Christmas, which is faith;
the warmth of Christmas, which is love;
the radiance of Christmas, which is purity;
the righteousness of Christmas, which is justice;
the belief in Christmas, which is truth;
the all of Christmas, which is Christ.

~ WILDA ENGLISH

See God in every person, place and thing, and all will be well in your world.

~ LOUISE L. HAY, SPEAKER
Author, www.louisehay.com

Be willing to believe in a greater way about yourself. Let your heart be receptive to God's Spirit and Guidance. Have the courage to make the decision to allow the possibility of greatness in you. Take risks beyond your boundaries, and God is right there with you.

~ MARY MANIN MORRISSEY
Author of Life Keys

I know God will not give me anything I can't handle.
I just wish that he didn't trust me so much.
~ MOTHER TERESA

It is Christmas every time you let God love others through you.
Yes, it is Christmas every time you smile at your brother and offer
him your hand.
~ MOTHER TERESA

Prayer is when you talk to God;
Meditation is when you listen to God.
~ DIANA ROBINSON

What you are is God's gift to you.
What you become is your gift to God.
~ ELEANOR ROOSEVELT

God can only do *for* you what he can do *through* you.
~ SHERYL ROUSH
Speaker, author of Sparkle-Tudes!
www.sparklepresentations.com

You can tell the size of your God by looking at the size of your worry list. The longer the list, the smaller your God.

~ UNKNOWN

If you believe in an unseen Christ, you will believe in the unseen Christ-like potential of others.

~ UNKNOWN

Do not make prayer a monologue—make it a conversation.

~ UNKNOWN

If I can do some good today,
If I can serve along life's way,
If I have something helpful to say,
Lord, show me how.
If I can right a human wrong,
If I can help to make one strong,
If I can cheer with smile or song,
Lord, show me how.
If I can aid one in distress,
If I can make a burden less,
If I can spread more happiness,
Lord, show me how.

~ UNKNOWN

A little faith will bring your soul to heaven,
but a lot of faith will bring heaven to your soul.
~ UNKNOWN

Because God is everywhere, you can pray anywhere.
~ UNKNOWN

The God that gives us life gives us the tools for our expansion and
is not responsible for how we use those tools.
~ JONI WILSON
Speaker, author of Wisdom Speaks to Women

What God intended for you goes far beyond anything you can
imagine.
~ OPRAH WINFREY

A little child,
A shining star,
A stable rude,
The door ajar.
Yet in that place,
So crude, forlorn,
The Hope of all the world was born.
~ UNKNOWN

CHRISTMAS CAROLING

*S*inging Christmas carols at the top of my lungs (even off-key but having fun), walking the neighborhoods with Camp Fire Girls, lead by my mother and Winona Grant, a most talented choral director. Lovely folks would actually come out of their homes, listen intently, sing along, and offer us hot chocolate, hot apple cider, and sugar cookies. Sure, some things have changed over the years. Neighbors don't know each other, let alone come out of the house to see who is at the door if even to greet them with holiday cheer and politically-correct religion-sensitive carols. Still, one of my Catholic-turned-Jewish inter-faithful friends, Dr. Teresa Shanahan, hosts an indoor chili dinner before thirty to forty of us head out into the brisk 50 to 60 degree Southern California beach air to sing carols (with strong flashlights, walking sticks, gloves, reading glasses, and song sheets in hand). She distributes notes to her neighbors in advance letting them know the day and time to expect us. Some are kind enough to have beer and spiced rum apple cider ready for our annual trek. I look forward to this so much every year, that I break out the Christmas song CDs and start listening to the words and tunes weeks in advance!

~ SHERYL ROUSH
Speaker, author, www.sparklepresentations.com

I love the Christmas-tide, and yet,
I notice this, each year I live;
I always like the gifts I get,
But how I love the gifts I give!

~ CAROLYN WELLS

MUSIC:
THE UNIVERSAL LANGUAGE OF THE HEART

*I*n spite of changes over the years, there remain some strong and beautiful universal threads in the tapestry of the Christmas season. These are found in the words of carols and songs that we know and cherish. The true meaning of Christmas is reflected in "Silent Night" or "Away in a Manger" and the importance of family and friends in "I'll Be Home for Christmas."

I don't remember there being any Spanish-speaking households at all in our small northern Illinois community back in the 1960s. That's what made it so fun and unique when our high school Spanish teacher arranged for members of her class to go out Christmas caroling—in Spanish! I still recall some of those songs over forty-five years later— "Noche de paz, noche de amor . . . " ("Silent Night").

~ CONNIE JAMESON

Christmas is the season when you buy this year's gifts with next year's money.

~ UNKNOWN

Once again, we come to the holiday season, a deeply religious time that each of us observes, in his own way, by going to the mall of his choice.

~ UNKNOWN

A New Christmas Song?

*T*he *Orange County Register Sun Post News* ran a story by Fred Swegles that caught my eye. On the front page was a young deer lying down, caught within the gate of someone's home. I just had to find out what happened to that little deer. As I read, I realized that the real story was about the little girl who was away at school at the time. She heard about the deer and was horrified. The little girl thought that Santa had surely sent the "reindeer" to deliver a special message to her. And now Santa would be mad. Well that did it. I had to write a song written from the perspective of the little girl. The first line came—"There's a Reindeer in my Gate." *P.S. The deer was okay and guided safely back up into the hills by the rescue team.*

There's A Reindeer in My Gate
Chorus
There's a reindeer in my gate
Santa don't be late
I haven't been bad
So don't get mad
I was still at school
When that little deer came through
When that little deer got stuck
Boy, what bum luck!
I was trying so hard to be
As good as I could be
Right there at my desk
Dreaming 'bout my Christmas tree
He was just a little fawn
Without his antlers on

(continued)

THERE'S A REINDEER IN MY GATE (CONTINUED)
It was just a baby reindeer
Trying to bring some Christmas cheer
Chorus
There's a reindeer on my lawn
A little stuck fawn
I knew he wasn't lost
He was sent by Santa Claus
He was trying to get in
A message he was deliverin'
When he couldn't get through
Now what should we do?
He just wanted to say "hi"
And so our gate he tried
But he must've eaten too much
That's why he got stuck
Chorus
I'm scared because
Maybe Santa Claus
Will cross me off his Christmas list
This isn't what I wished!
So my mommy called some reindeer friends
To get him off that gate
'Cause we didn't want to take a chance
That Santa would be late
Then my mommy told the deer
That they would soon be here
She said, "Honey don't you worry,
Little deer don't cry

(continued)

THERE'S A REINDEER IN MY GATE (CONTINUED)
It'll only be a minute
'Til help comes by"
When those officers got here
To save the little deer
They pulled that reindeer out
And not by his snout
Chorus
They got my reindeer free
And I was so happy
Now that reindeer could tell Santa Claus
It was not my fault
It ran down the street
Then it ran away
Now it wouldn't have to pull a gate
Just Santa's sleigh
Up through the canyon
Back to the North Pole
But I wished there were a message
To the deer I had told
I would've said . . .
Chorus
"Bye my little reindeer friend"
This is what I'd say
Next time you come to say hello . . .
Could you come on Saturday?"

~ TERRI MARIE
Author of Be the Hero of Your Own Game,
and The Solution is at Hand: The Dottie Walters Story
www.spiritualarena.com
© 2005

At work every year, my company participates in the Angel Project. An Angel purchases a gift for a needy child based on age and gender. We have an idea of what the child would like to receive as a gift. I select children that are the ages of my grandchildren, then I plan a shopping trip with the kids that is entirely focused on gifts for the project. The rule is that everything we buy is for the Angel children. With all the abundance we have in our lives, I feel strongly that our children can learn about giving early in life. The kids look forward to a day with Grandma and they love shopping for other children.

~ LAUREN KELLY

Love awaits you
From inside out
From outside in
The abundance of love is recognized
In the thoughts we have
In the deeds we do
In simply showing up
Love awaits you

~ TINA MERTEL

Never worry about the size of your Christmas tree. In the eyes of children, they are all thirty feet tall.

~ LARRY WILDE
The Merry Book of Christmas

LAST-MINUTE SHOPPING

I was the oldest of seven children. Our family tradition was to open the Christmas gifts from each other and our relatives on Christmas Eve, so there would be room for Santa's gifts in the morning. Well, my husband and I were busy going to college and working jobs; plus, we lived out-of-town; plus, I must admit, we were "pokey." We never seemed to complete our shopping until the last minute. We'd then drive home on Christmas Eve, our car weighed down with gifts for my mom, dad, and six little brothers and sisters— and wrapping paper, ribbon, scissors and tape!

My poor younger siblings would have to wait downstairs, while my husband and I went upstairs to complete the wrapping of all those gifts. Finally, after what must have seemed like hours to them, we finally came down the stairs, arms loaded with our wrapped presents—that would then be almost immediately unwrapped!

Now, more than forty years later, I am still occasionally reminded of the "cruel and unusual punishment" we inflicted on my little brothers and sisters all those Christmas Eves long, long ago.

~ CONNIE JAMESON

I sometimes think we expect too much of Christmas Day. We try to crowd into it the long arrears of kindliness and humanity of the whole year. As for me, I like to take my Christmas a little at a time, all through the year. And thus I drift along into the holidays—let them overtake me unexpectedly—waking up some fine morning and suddenly saying to myself: "Why, this is Christmas Day!"

~ DAVID GRAYSON

Christmas! 'Tis the season for kindling the fire of hospitality in the hall, the genial fire of charity in the heart.

~ WASHINGTON IRVING

The joy of brightening other lives, bearing each others' burdens, easing other's loads, and supplanting empty hearts and lives with generous gifts becomes for us the magic of Christmas.

~ W.C. JONES

The only real blind person at Christmastime is he who has not Christmas in his heart.

~ HELEN KELLER

MIDNIGHT MASS

*O*ur special night had come! My older sister Alice and I had waited many years for it to arrive!

Our household had been large one—my mother and father, four aunts and uncles, Alice, and me. We all lived together in our cozy two-story home in Erie, Pennsylvania. My parents had taken in my aunts and uncles when they were young to keep them out of an orphanage after their mother's death. At that time, Alice and I were babies.

As we all grew, there was love and laughter in our home. We enjoyed all the holidays, but my mother somehow always made Christmas even more special. Once they grew up and married, my aunts and uncles moved into their own homes, but on Christmas Eve, they and their families returned, just like old times, to celebrate with us.

Our house was surrounded by a variety of churches for blocks in every direction. On Christmas Eve, what a glorious sound it was when all their different bells rang out! That was when my parents and all the others would go to Midnight Mass, but sadly, my sister and I were too young to attend. After the service, our house would fill to the seams with relatives; eating, laughing, exchanging gifts, telling stories, playing music. Still too young to be allowed to take part, Alice and I would tip-toe quietly down the stairs in our pajamas, like two tiny mice. We'd be oh-so-quiet, so no one could catch us peeping at all the festivities through the slot in the dining room door frame.

She and I could hardly wait to get older, so we could join in on all that love, food, and fun. Year after year, we would creep down those stairs, watching and waiting for that magical day to come. Eventually, we grew into our early teens, and that special day arrived. We were finally allowed to attend Midnight Mass on Christmas Eve! That was a gift in itself!

(continued)

MIDNIGHT MASS (CONTINUED)

The mass was even more majestic and holy than I had ever believed it would be. St. Ann's Church, where all our family attended, was beautifully adorned with flowers– glowing red poinsettias on the main altar, side altars, everywhere. The reverent voices from the choir drifted down to my ears, and I planned then that someday I would sing in that same choir to pay holy tribute to our Savior's birth. I felt blessed to finally be part of it all.

After mass came an even more magical time. Bells from all the churches were still ringing so clearly that they could be heard for miles, their joyous sounds drifting out onto the dark night air. As we headed home, enormous white snowflakes were falling, thickening the sky with their brilliance. The air was brisk, but not bitter cold.

The most special part of it all was walking home with my father. He was a big man, with huge hands, thickly calloused from years of hard work in a factory. As we all walked along, he tucked my small cold hand into his large warm one. With my short legs, I tried to match his footsteps stride-for-stride, to be in tandem as we walked. When our footsteps finally matched side-by-side in the snow, I felt united with him as never before. As our house came into view, there in the front window was our sparkling Christmas tree, lovingly and beautifully decorated by my mother, waiting to welcome us in.

It was truly special that I was now old enough to join all the others in attending the mass, and the festivities of food and opening gifts afterwards. But still the most outstanding part of that evening was walking home with my father. We had been hand-in-hand, heart-to-heart, all the way from the church to our house. It's a memory that's as fresh in my mind today as it was those many years ago; one that I will cherish forever.

~ KAY PRESTO

THE SCRAPBOOK OF MY MIND

A camera preserves memories, holiday memories we hope we never lose. My first camera was a Yashica 35 millimeter FX electronic beauty. Not only was it superbly crafted for the neophyte, it was special. It was a gift from my older brother who brought it home after his tour of duty in Vietnam. That camera always had a nose for capturing the perfect moments, moments when my family would get together for Christmas dinner.

To preserve those moments, all I had to do was load a roll of ASA 100 color film and focus, aim, and click. When the target was correctly framed, the Yashica lit up like a Christmas tree. Then it would deliver bright, rich, keepsake family memories that were priceless. It never failed me. Too bad I failed it.

It was Christmas Day. I was the youngest child . . . two years younger than my sister, seven years younger than my older brother, and eight years younger than my oldest brother.

Every Christmas Day we met at my mother's house for a Texas-sized dinner. It was a tradition that would last for my mother's lifetime. No matter where we lived, we always found a pathway to her house on Christmas Day. It was a special time. A time to be thankful for who we were and grateful for what we had. And a time to pig out on Mama's cooking! What a love affair that was.

With a love no measuring cup could hold; she baked her cakes, pies, cookies, turkey and dressing, and ham with all the trimmings. We always had a royal feast worthy of capturing on film. That's exactly what I did. This one particular Christmas was extra rich with memorable moments. That was because I captured a lot of pictures of my mother on film.

(continued)

THE SCRAPBOOK OF MY MIND (CONTINUED)

She rarely allowed pictures to be taken of her. But on this day I had thirty-six snapshots! Moments that would be cherished for a lifetime. It when I returned to California after the Christmas holidays that I realized the horrible error.

I opened up the camera to remove my treasured film only to discover that the film never advanced. I was devastated. The great moments I thought I captured were never transferred to film. That opportunity would never come again. Those memories were lost.

Well, that's what I thought. I now understand that great memories aren't captured, they are recovered. When I relax, release, and reflect through the scrapbook of my mind, I find those lost images not snapped by a camera. It made me realize that treasured moments are not recreated in a dark room by human hands; they are recovered from the safety chambers of the human heart where they have been beautifully framed and neatly tucked away so they can never be erased. That's one thing I remember about Christmas.

~ JIM TUCKER
Speaker, author

CHRISTMAS BOOTS
AND SWEET TOOTHS

*M*om made felt-decorated Christmas boots instead of stockings. They were made out of old Maxwell House coffee cans. When times were lean they were filled with walnuts, oranges, and large Brazil nuts. Sweet tooths run in my family tree for generations back. I think that we could have family reunions that only have potluck desserts—skip the main courses—and we'd all be happy campers! My grandmother's cookies from the Iowa farm were the best around. My mother always made the best fresh pies and holiday fudges. It should be an Olympic sport—making fluffy "White Divinity Fudge." The secret to whether it's going to fluff or flop is how long it boils. I remember her even making home-made peanut brittle, black walnut maple fudge, and popcorn balls. Today I bring chocolate-dipped Ritz crackers with peanut butter inside, or frosted kahlua white chip macademia Brownies . . . and the new favorite from the Hawaiian family members is "Moose Munch"—chocolate covered blueberries! Regardless of the gifts, the chocolates are opened with reverence, and quickly devoured or inhaled, as I've observed. Making and eating desserts is definitely one of our favorite traditions!

~ SHERYL ROUSH
Speaker, author, www.sparklepresentations.com

IN THREE WORDS

Memories, flashbacks,
celebrations
Kisses under mistletoe
Cheery red cheeks
Children wide-eyed
Excited laughing children
Frantic rushing parents
Presents under trees
Receiving favorite things
Proposals and rings
Families traveling far
Driving loaded cars
Sweet hot chocolate
Candy cane treats
Apple rum cider
Nutmeg and eggnog
Making plans early
Late night parties
Singing holiday tunes
Cherished friends' reunion
Love abundantly shared
Long airplane flights
Snowed-in delays
Families lovingly reunited

Tears of joy
Cats batting ornaments
Dogs chasing cats
Lights flickering on
Angels atop trees
Sweet treats galore
Frosting sugar cookies
Dipping cheese balls
Avoiding fruit cakes
Exchanging holiday recipes
Joyous carols sung
Hope-filled stockings hung
Crisp snowflakes fall
Card sentiments mailed
Monthly earnings spent
Playing in snow
Sparkling garland shines
Shopping last minute
World peace rings
Packing it up
Storing it away
Waiting another year
Anticipating next year
Doing it again

~ SHERYL ROUSH
Speaker, author, www.sparklepresentations.com

CHRISTMAS IN ANDALUCÍA

*C*hristmas away from hearth, home, and family—no way! Yet, twenty-five years ago I spent not one, but three Christmas seasons in southern Spain. My Navy husband, our three-month-old son and I had moved to the small town of Rota, near Sevilla, in the province of Andalucía for a three-year tour of duty.

What do most Americans do when faced with spending a holiday away from family and cherished traditions? We try to create a "home away from home" and all our traditions seem all the more important. My first dash of reality was trying to find a Christmas tree. I stubbornly held to my idea of a fresh cut tree, but low and behold, such a thing did not exist in southern Spain. No Christmas tree lots magically appeared, and even a thorough search through a few plant nurseries came up short. However, the Navy Exchange came through with an artificial tree of the bottle brush variety with the little plastic trunk.

The Christmas tree hunt made me realize that I should open my eyes to find out how Christmas was celebrated in Spain rather than to get bound up in my own expectations.

Many moments come to mind as I think back to sitting in an ancient Catholic church one evening in December. I was listening to a beautiful pipe organ concert while sitting on a cold hard pew, in a dark and chilly stone sanctuary, and feeling God's presence filling the space.

On Christmas Eve, everyone in town was out on foot streaming, as if drawn by a magnet, toward the town square outside the church. As we drew closer, the crowds became so thick that we put my little fifteen-month-old son up on his dad's shoulders to give him a vantage point as well as to shelter him from the crowd.

(continued)

CHRISTMAS IN ANDALUCÍA (CONTINUED)

The whole town it seemed was crowded into the square, pressed in like a rock concert, but yet subdued and reverent to celebrate the birth of Christ.

In Spain, Christmas is not all wrapped up in gift giving the way we are in America. Christmas is its own celebration and the gift giving is done 12 days later on Three Kings Day—January 6th. This is cause for a whole new celebration as everyone takes to the streets again for the annual parade, a fabulous display with the kings riding atop floats and hordes of attendants dressed in costume accompanying them. The whole town pulsates with the excitement of the gala atmosphere.

Years later, I fondly treasure the exotic memories of celebrating Christmas abroad. While I still like the old, familiar traditions, I know that keeping my mind and heart open to experience the joy that is around us wherever we are is the true meaning of Christmas!

~ LINNEA BLAIR

I BELIEVE IN SANTA CLAUS
I believe in Santa Claus.
I believe there's always hope when all seems lost.
And I believe in Santa Claus,
I believe in Santa Claus, I'll tell you why I do.
'Cause I believe that dreams and plans and wishes can come true.
I believe in miracles, I believe in magic too.
Oh I believe in Santa Claus and I believe in you.

~ LYRICS (PARTIAL HERE) BY DOLLY PARTON
Sung with Kenny Rogers on the album. Once Upon A Christmas

MY PRETTY SANTA

They say that Santa's jolly, and has a long white beard;
They say he wears a red suit, and brings gifts every year.
But now that I am older, and see things much more clear,
I'll tell you all a secret, if you will all draw near.
My Santa is so pretty, so loving and so dear;
She'll stay up half the night, to see us smile from ear to ear.
When others are too busy, or simply are not there;
She'll bake and shop and wrap just right, to bring us Christmas cheer.
She knows just what we want, her goal is very clear,
Her loving hands work tirelessly to make Christmas magically appear.
With her lonely, thankless task complete, candy; dolls;
toys and miscellaneous gear;
Bright and early Christmas morn, "Santa came" is all we hear.
And I'll be ever grateful, my wish for her sincere;
God Bless my Santa-Mom, as she has blessed us through the years!

~ RITA LANELL SHAW DE LOS REYES
Age 13 at time of writing

Editor's note: Today Rita is a mother of three, and grandmother of six.

Once again we find ourselves enmeshed in the holiday season, that very special time of year when we join with our loved ones in sharing centuries-old traditions such as trying to find a parking space at the mall. We traditionally do this in my family by driving around the parking lot until we see a shopper emerge from the mall, then we follow her, in very much the same spirit as the Three Wise Men, who 2,000 years ago followed a star, week after week, until it led them to a parking space.

~ DAVE BARRY

When my daughter was about five years old, she was not settling down to go to sleep. It was close to Christmas time, so I told her to be good and go to sleep, because Santa was watching her.

She asked, "Where is he?" and I replied "He is everywhere." I pointed to the window. "He might even be on that light pole outside your window watching you."

She looked at me very seriously and said, "Close the curtain."

~ SHIRLIE CUNNINGHAM

Roses are reddish
Violets are bluish
If it weren't for Christmas
We'd all be Jewish.

~ BENNY HILL

THE SANTA SACK

*A*s a very young kid, I don't remember getting a Christmas stocking each year. It wasn't until junior high or high school, when one year my mom made stockings for my sister, brother, me, daddy, and herself. They turned out to be huge. Mom later said she had a hard time filling them.

The next year, we were in for another surprise; our stockings had been cut in half lengthwise and sewn onto the outside of a very large Santa Sack! Now there were seven stockings! All our Santa gifts were in the sack with the stockings sewn onto the outside. The stockings had our initials sewn onto them in sequins and yes, there were a couple of stockings with no initials. Even cut in half the stockings seemed large. From then on, the Santa Sack made its appearance every year at Christmas. Even though I knew better, it still felt like Santa left his sack especially for us each year.

As our family grew with in-laws and grandkids, nieces and nephews, the Santa Sack expanded to include everyone. After all seven of the stockings had initials, we began sharing stockings or giving ours up to the next generation of children. We got creative with the initials too. Some of us shared stockings. If the new person's name didn't start with an already existing initial, we would devise a way to make it work.

During the Christmas holidays in the late 60s, mom was in the hospital recuperating from a mastectomy. On Christmas Day, we filled the Santa Sack with gifts, drove to the hospital, and celebrated Christmas with mom in her room. Daddy had my brother carry the sack into mom's room in the hospital. That was a special Christmas. Mom had made that sack for all of us and now we were able to give it back to her and help brighten her Christmas.

(continued)

THE SANTA SACK (CONTINUED)

The Santa Sack has never missed a Christmas in forty years, and is now getting ready to create special memories for the next generation. After my parents died, I ended up with the sack. Now, when I spend Christmas with any of my grand-nieces and nephews I'll take the Santa Sack with me. I can't wait to see the look of amazement on their faces when they see Santa's Sack at their house!

When I decorate for the holidays, I love taking the Santa Sack out and remembering all the years it's been in use. It brings back such wonderful memories of family.

~ CAROLYNN BRAMLETT

The Supreme Court has ruled that they cannot have a nativity scene in Washington, D.C. This wasn't for any religious reasons. They couldn't find three wise men and a virgin.

~ JAY LENO

SANTA'S ELF

When my girls still believed in Santa Claus, I often had gifts I wanted them to have for use before Christmas. Things like pretty dresses for holiday parties or trips to the *Nutcracker* ballet, or warm colorful jackets for pre-Christmas trips to Disneyland. I found a wonderful solution to this Christmas present dilemma. Santa had an elf who occasionally dropped things off early for good little girls. His name was Eelrac.

Eelrac left the wrapped presents on the girls' beds and a note taped to the bedroom door. Something on the order of "Eelrac was here," or in subsequent years, "Eelrac strikes again!" Rebecca and Rachel were often more delighted by the surprise visit than the gifts themselves. The elf became something they would talk about in anticipation starting around Thanksgiving, wondering if Eelrac would come this year. Long after they outgrew Santa, they pined for Eelrac. Eventually he became a Christmas tradition, always showing up just in time with things better used before than after Christmas, like new Christmas ornaments, warm gloves, or party shoes. It wasn't until they were teenagers that they realized what Eelrac's name was when spelled backwards!

Eelrac has become a special holiday tradition between me and my girls, one we all look forward to every year. Even now with both girls in college, you never know when or where, but Eelrac still strikes!

~ CARLEE WESTBROOK

THE CHRISTMAS SPIES

*J*im, my little brother, and I were very curious to see just how Santa managed to get himself down our chimney. I was five years old and Jim was four. I had a plan that I worked on for weeks to spy on this mysterious event.

Every year, my frugal parents would purchase a Christmas tree that was only about four feet tall. To make it look like a "grand" tall tree, they placed it on top of a sturdy square coffee table. The table was first covered with an old sheet draped down the sides and onto the floor.

My plan was for us to hide under this coffee table and wait for the sacred moment of Santa's arrival. We'd see it with our own eyes! We practiced sneaking under the coffee table, positioning ourselves to get comfortable, curling up for hours of waiting we knew were ahead of us. We practiced many times leading up to December 25th, without our parents ever catching on to what we were scheming. My brother was clever enough to bring some snacks that night in case we got hungry. This was our big secret. It is still a part of the bonding I now have with my brother.

The big night arrived. We could hear our parents talking late in their room. We tiptoed past their room unnoticed, and then ran to the living room where the big event would occur. I remember my heart pounding with excitement in anticipation that this was the real thing. This was what we had planned and practiced for. It was very hard not to tell others what we had planned but we knew if we were to get a glimpse of Santa, no one could know. Somehow, we just had a feeling that it was taboo to trick Santa.

(continued)

THE CHRISTMAS SPIES (CONTINUED)

We were under the table for a while when my brother fell asleep. I must have fallen asleep shortly after he did. We woke to the sound of our parents yelling for us when they did not find us in our beds. I soon found out that my return answers went unheard and we were trapped.

You see, Santa not only came, but he left lots of big toys and presents all around the coffee table. Most of them were placed on that sheet that draped down over the sides and onto the carpet. This not only muffled our replies but made it very difficult for us to get out from under the table. We were shocked that Santa had come. We not only missed seeing him but he may not have even realized he was putting the presents right next to where we were hiding from him.

Our parents were speechless once they found us. Later that day, they demanded the full story. I was not sure if they were laughing or crying. Now that I am a parent, I look back and know they had to be filled with laughter at the antics of their Christmas spies.

~ PATTY ANDERSON

SAVING CHRISTMAS

*M*elancholic feelings flooded my head driving home one Christmas evening with my husband and his son. Had I made the wrong decision, was I being selfish, should I have addressed the situation earlier? My stepson was well over ten years old and wasn't really sure about the whole Santa idea. For the past seven years, I had prepared for Christmas by myself—shopping, decorating, cooking, baking, and planning parties. This year my husband and I were having problems and I decided that I was not going to do it—instead waiting to see if anything would happen without me.

When we walked into our home my stepson looked under the tree, then up to me with those beautiful, sad, almost tearful eyes and said with conviction, "There are not many presents under the tree." My heart broke as I realized I had made a bad choice. It was not my stepson's fault I was angry. I glanced over at my husband, tears welling in my eyes then back to my stepson. In my cheeriest voice I replied, "Well, you know how I'm always late. Santa probably knew that we would be gone for Christmas so I bet he'll come tomorrow." Pretty lame, but it was all I could come up with, "Yeah, right" was the response.

The day after Christmas and all the after-Christmas sales; could I salvage the last year my stepson actually believed in Santa? I vowed to try my hardest. After breakfast and setting Ashton up with a movie, I told him I was off to the grocery store. Since he knew how much I like to cook, this was an acceptable alibi. I hit the store at super speed, Mach force, and with the voracity of a mad woman. While I was keeping Ashton busy with various chores, I would run in the bedroom and wrap presents.

(continued)

SAVING CHRISTMAS (CONTINUED)

When I came out, Ashton suggested that just in case Santa came maybe we should put out the animals stockings too so they wouldn't be forgotten. Oh my gosh! More shopping for the critters. Could he actually still believe this was going to happen? I HAD to make it come true.

Ring, ring . . . pick up, pick up, *pleezeee*! My neighbor finally answered. "Yes, I know this is a strange request, but what are neighbors for? Just because you pretend to be a grumpy old man doesn't mean you are. I need your help to play Santa tonight." Of course he had to remind me what day it was and ask me if I was crazy.

I explained the scenario to my neighbor, The Grinch. "We will be going to dinner at 6:30 P.M. and we will return between 8-8:30 P.M. All the presents are wrapped and labeled and ready to go under the tree. There are separate bags for the stockings with everyone's name on them. The fire is set, just light it, put out the milk, cookies, and carrots for Santa and the reindeer. Oh and put the iced champagne, sparkling cider, and glasses in front of the fireplace. Don't forget to turn the Christmas tree lights on so Ashton can see under the tree—the rest of the house lights should be off. Got it? Any questions?"

"Do you *really* think this is going to work? Do you *really* think he is going to believe it?"

"How can he not?" was my response. "We'll both be at dinner with him—who else would come into our house and do this unless they were crazy?" My friend said I had a valid point.

As we headed for home I could sense the anticipation. Although Ashton had not mentioned anything I knew he was hoping, wishing, and praying for it to happen.

(continued)

SAVING CHRISTMAS (CONTINUED)

The outdoor lights were still on. The indoor lights were off except for a slight flicker from the tree. As we entered the house, Ashton bolted for the tree. Screaming in delight, he announced that Santa had indeed visited us while we were at dinner.

I say, "That's crazy, it's not possible."

He grabs my hand and pulls me over to the tree. Presents everywhere. "*Look!* The stockings are full, the fire is lit—*he came*! You were right."

And that, folks, is how I made one little boy very happy and saved myself from disbelieving; even if sometimes you don't want to believe in the magic. It is always there and more often than not, it is closer than you could possibly imagine. May you always find the magic in the season.

~ TERESA KUFFEL

I once bought my kids a set of batteries for Christmas with a note on it saying, toys not included.

~ BERNARD MANNING

THE PHANTOM SANTA

*I*f I were to pick one period of our lives that could stand as a symbol of love, sharing, friendship and in fact, the very personification of the teaching and life of that little babe born in Bethlehem so long ago, it would have to be the Christmas of 1979.

It had been a year filled with stressful situations and some major changes in our lives. My husband had made the courageous decision to change careers at midlife and return to school. After much soul searching and prayer, we had decided to move to Missoula, Montana, buy a home, go to graduate school full time and live on our savings.

So in April 1979, when we moved into our home with five daughters, we unpacked our hopes and dreams along with the dishes and bed linen. But as the saying goes, "Life is what happens to you after you have made your plans." A lot of those plans and strategies that looked so good on paper, in reality were not materializing.

The ensuing months brought us a larger than usual share of disappointments and financial burdens. We were facing Christmas with a rapidly diminishing savings account and we were far away from families and old friends.

Because we were active in church, school and community groups, we had met many people and were just beginning to feel our roots sink in and take hold. But we had not cemented any special, forever after type of friendships that we felt secure enough in to share our fears, loneliness and frustrations. Trying as hard as we could to remain optimistic, we were beginning to question our decision to move to Missoula.

(continued)

THE PHANTOM SANTA (CONTINUED)

On December 13, my husband and I had gone shopping and upon returning home found some very excited and wide-eyed children. It seems that the front doorbell had rung and when the girls ran to answer it, they found no one there. Mystified, they decided to check the back door and found a huge, wrapped box. The contents of the box were small gifts for everyone and the biggest surprise of all—a letter from Santa. I don't remember the entire poem, but part of it said:

"On the twelve days of Christmas, my true love gave to me
Gifts galore and lots of surprises,
Delivered by Santa in many disguises.
You can look all around, but you'll never see
Who's delivering a present to you from me."

And that is exactly what happened for the next eleven days. We received a gift every day. The gifts were not expensive, but showed real thought and caring. For instance, there was a box covered with contact paper for our eight year old to keep barrettes in, and the ingredients for chocolate chip cookies.

The presents were almost incidental to the fun we had trying to catch our phantom Santa. But he/she/they used ingenious methods of delivery. Gifts were left on the front seat of the car, in the mailbox and at the neighbors. One gift was even delivered by a foreign student, who spoke no English (or so he claimed).

The game became an analytical one. Who loved us so much that they would go to all that trouble? Was it this neighbor or that one? Was it a teacher from school or a co-worker? Was it someone from the bank or from church?

(continued)

THE PHANTOM SANTA (CONTINUED)

How could we ever thank them if we didn't know who or why they were being so loving and generous? We began looking at others with a more open spirit. Thinking that it must be this one or that one, we went out of our way to be loving and kind to all those with whom we came in contact. When confronted and questioned, our friends and acquaintances all denied knowledge of the phantom Santa, but all agreed it was a wonderful idea.

Soon we noticed that the sunshine and love that we felt were being passed around faster than a midwinter cold. Smiles were bigger and greetings were merrier. Hearts and minds became more reflective on the true meaning of Christmas as those questioned almost universally said, "No, it isn't us, but I wish it were."

We never did know for sure who our phantom Santa was, even though we had a pretty good idea. We will forever be grateful to that family who gave us so much that year—a fun-filled Christmas season, some true gifts of the spirit, the basis for forming everlasting friendships as well as a tradition for our family to carry on.

But, best of all, was the stamp of approval on our decision to make Missoula, Montana our home and to give back to the community that had welcomed us so warmly.

~ JUDY H. WRIGHT
Speaker, author, www.artichokepress.com
© 2001 Judy H. Wright

DEAR SANTA CLAUS
When I was young and childish,
I sent you Christmas lists,
Of toys and games and fun-filled things,
For which I dearly wished.
You did not bring me everything,
But you never let me down,
Though I was young, I understood,
You had to spread your gifts around.
Eventually my letters stopped,
Somewhere I learned the score,
Besides that I grew too old,
To believe in Santa anymore.
But this year, Santa, I've decided,
To take out my pad and pen,
To give you another try,
And write you once again.
So, dear Santa, please find enclosed,
My brand new Christmas list,
These are the things I want this year,
This is my new wish-list.

(continued)

(CONTINUED)

First, since I am older now,
And can look beyond myself,
I see no need for cutesy things,
To display upon a shelf.
Instead, items of the heart now,
Are what I earnestly request,
Though how you'll Christmas wrap them,
I can't begin to guess.
How can you package friendship,
Or put wrappings around love,
Or tie ribbons to a smile,
Or hang holly from a hug?
Can The Golden Rule be wrapped in silver,
Or The Ten Commandments tied with gold?
Can prayers be cushioned in a box,
And what about a hand to hold?
I think caring, sharing attitudes,
Are lovely presents, too,
And gracious generosities,
Of time and purse are cool.
World peace is something else,
Though I suppose that makes you laugh,

(continued)

(CONTINUED)

But, oh Santa, how we need it,
And it does no harm to ask.
I know you cannot wrap these things,
In colored paper and with bows,
Or hang them from a Christmas tree,
Or place them down below.
I don't know how you'll hand them out,
But these things I've mentioned here,
Are on my list for Christmas,
For my friends and me this year.
It's a funny list, I know,
I suspect you'll scratch your head,
I guess I ought to go to God,
For these are gifts of his, instead,
These items are God's blessings,
And I really do know better,
So, Santa, perhaps the thing to do,
Is throw away this letter.
God's causes are not Santa Claus',
But you should understand,
Although God doesn't really need it,
He sure loves an extra hand!

~ VIRGINIA (GINNY) ELLIS
www.poetrybyginny.com
© *December 2002*

HOME IS WHERE THE HEART IS

*S*ometimes our greatest fear is returning to the house in which were raised, or at least it was for me. The house represents where we gained our identity, raised by our primary caregivers. We learned about life, others, love, and ourselves. It's the house itself. It's the countless and significant early childhood memories developed there.

Even though I live only a seventeen-minute drive away from the house where I was raised, I feel strange when returning, even to visit my parents, or deliver items to them. Since I no longer live there, I feel as if I'm a guest. At age twenty, I couldn't wait to move out—get my own apartment, and "a life" of my own.

That changes—or my feelings regarding it—at the holidays. The youngest of three, and still referred to lovingly by my mother as her "baby," I find myself reverting into the role of Mama's Little Helper around the house when company comes, even when it's only one of my brothers. I feel reconnected to the house, the family, and become the "Hostess with the Mostess," as my father always called me.

Setting the table, clearing the table, "cheering up the dishes," bringing additional bags of groceries over to share unique international food items and elegant wines that I know everyone will enjoy. From salsa and poppy seed tortilla chips, decadent chocolates, hummus blends, dried fruits and sweets galore . . . close and extended family comes from near and far to share their stories.

Today, I see the old house where I grew up as a welcoming place. A home where my brothers can always return and share with their families.

(continued)

HOME IS WHERE THE HEART IS (CONTINUED)

When my father designed the homestead (a fantastic feat for a military design engineer checker with no architectural background), he truly was designing a home for his family for generations. Still today, my brothers' bedrooms are decorated with sports awards and medals hanging on the walls from their childhood as if inspiration for their aspiring children, each with a story their father will gladly share at a moment's notice, offering an inkling into their parents' lives. Favorite photographs and magazines (*National Geographic*) adorn the room, which perhaps served as inspiration for my own life, traveling the globe.

Yet wherever I travel, I love coming home.

At the holidays, the meaning of coming home is so much more clear, more sacred, more near and dear to one's heart. It's true, as Dorothy claimed in the *Wizard of Oz*, "There's no place like home." I know the truth, that home IS where the heart is.

~ SHERYL ROUSH
Author, speaker, www.sparklepresentations.com

CHRISTMAS IS . . .
Christmas is a lot of things,
To many different folks,
Yet to most it means the same,
The renewal of men's hopes.

It is the celebration,
Of the baby Jesus' birth,
When men sing of his creation,
And pray for peace on earth.

It's when people kneel in gratitude,
To the good Lord up above,
When they declare to Him in prayer,
Their dedication and their love.

It's when folks forgive their fellowmen,
For the wrongs they have perceived,
And when men also seek forgiveness
For their errors and misdeeds.

Christmas is a time of magic,
For one's close friends and family,
A time of warm togetherness,
Of reality and fantasy.

(continued)

(CONTINUED)

Christmas is the tree we see,
With its packages below,
It's the smiling angel at its top,
And the sparkling lights that glow.

It's the wreath that hangs upon the door,
It's the caroling we hear.
It's the fun-filled thoughts of Santa Claus,
And the visions of his deer.

It's the cold night air of Christmas Eve,
It's the promised Christmas snow,
It's the grin upon a snowman's face,
And his funny carrot nose.
Christmas is when people laugh,
It is also when they cry,
And so fine the line that's in between,
It can't be seen by the human eye.

Christmas is the past and present,
Brought together for awhile,
Something old and something new,
A blend of tears and smiles.

~ VIRGINIA (GINNY) ELLIS
www.poetrybyginny.com
© December 2004

A NEW CHRISTMAS LEGEND

They say it happened at Christmas time. And that makes sense, since retail is so crazy in December. The situation between the Sears store manager, Jack Mills, and his assistant, Daniel Watter, grew ugly and tense. Mills was an old-style autocrat who thought his ideas were always the best and Watter, a younger, better-looking up-and-comer, wanted what was best for the nation's number one retailer. Remember, this was before the days of super huge discount stores and at this time, nobody did retail better than Sears.

Not only did Watter have a wife who shopped a lot and a little girl who had the "wishbook" memorized, he also conducted surveys and market research. He knew what triggered customer buying decisions. He placated angry consumers. He inspired loyalty among employees and he set a good example, getting to the store hours before it opened, just to make sure the floors were clean and displays straight.

Maybe it was envy or fear, but Jack Mills didn't appreciate his right-hand man's productivity and ideas. He belittled Daniel in front of department managers, and once in front of a middle-aged blonde applying for a credit card. Daniel and the woman were both embarrassed.

This Christmas, the Sears store was under enormous pressure from corporate headquarters to increase profits 20 percent over the previous year. In fact, there was a rumor that if the store didn't do at least that well, it would be closed and replaced with what's called a catalog venue. That means people could buy a few big appliances and everything else they wanted would have to be ordered from the Sears catalog. Daniel was challenged by the mandate to increase profits. He authorized special newspaper advertisements and even dressed as Santa Claus one afternoon when the real Santa drank too much at lunch.

(continued)

A NEW CHRISTMAS LEGEND (CONTINUED)

Daniel's efforts seemed to be working. A "midnight madness" sale on December 15th doubled revenue for the first half of the month. In departmental meetings, Daniel inspired workers and hinted at the desperate reason higher sales were needed. He was pleased that staffers promised to do better than ever. But it worried the young supervisor that his boss didn't appear to care about results, only about criticizing.

There was the Christmas window display incident. Daniel had instructed the window dresser to "make magic." The dresser created the most imaginative window seen in the small city. It was called *Grandma's Attic—Year 2000.* Since this about two decades before the turn of the century, the attic was full of goodies for sale now.

Citizens loved the display. Jack Mills hated it. Mills told Daniel it was too space-age, made shoppers think too hard, and didn't attract buyers. Despite Daniel's protests that the creative front window had brought new customers into the store, Mills ended the discussion abruptly by telling the assistant manager he'd better "watch it or else."

Daniel was confused. Was Mills threatening him with his job? Daniel was trying to be the best assistant manager he could. Sales were high, traffic was up, and the store had never looked better. Besides, Daniel, a team player and professional, did his best to make Mills look good. He never argued with him in front of others and when he did disagree with Mills, he did so politely and respectfully and only to help the store, never to make Mills look bad.

Daniel tried to put Mills' warning out of his mind. After all, it was December and he didn't have time to worry about it. Chicago needed extra Chatty Cathy's and the Dallas regional distribution center wanted Baby First Step's.

(continued)

A NEW CHRISTMAS LEGEND (CONTINUED)

A customer was threatening a lawsuit if gift wrapping didn't hurry, and a kid had just peed on the mattress display. Plus, Daniel had to call Bobby, the window dresser, in from the district office to come change that display.

One day in the midst of the hustle and bustle, Daniel realized it was December 23rd and he hadn't bought his family any gifts. He called his wife and asked, "Honey, what are we going to do about Christmas?"

She laughed, "Haven't you noticed the tree and all of the gifts?"

Rather than admit he hadn't, Daniel countered, "Well, what about my gift for you?"

She, loving him for remembering on December 23rd this year, not on the 25th as he did on most years, answered, "I've already taken care of that. But I don't have Carrie's Santa Claus gifts yet. Can you buy some toys tomorrow night on your way home?"

She was referring to the gifts that appeared Christmas morning from Santa Claus. Daniel's daughter Carrie was six and still believed in the old guy. Daniel would be glad when he could get the praise and hugs and credit that were now bestowed on Santa Claus.

After promising to pick up a few items, Daniel hung up and went back on the sales floor. The store would close at ten tonight, and at six tomorrow night, Christmas Eve.

At about 4 P.M. on the 24th, Daniel collected cash register receipts and determined sales for December were 28 percent ahead of last year's. If after-Christmas returns weren't horrible, the store would easily meet its mandate and stay alive for at least another year. No one would be laid-off and the city would keep its department store. Daniel walked the aisles, congratulating and thanking the department managers for their hard work.

(continued)

A NEW CHRISTMAS LEGEND (CONTINUED)

At about 5:50 P.M., Daniel remembered the toys he was supposed to buy. He didn't want to keep the employees in that department after work, so he hurried.

"Whatcha got left that a little girl might like, Jose?" Daniel asked the toy department clerk.

"It's pretty picked over, Mr. Watter. But we've already started marking sale prices, so you can get some good deals."

"Great," Daniel commented. And because his spirits were so high, he selected lots: a miniature electric typewriter and a tiny sewing machine, a giant stuffed frog, a dollhouse, a few Hot Wheels and many Barbie outfits. His daughter hadn't seen much of him this month, so she might as well reap the reward of having a dad in retail.

As Daniel was signing the credit card slip with the employee 10 percent discount, Jack Mills walked up.

"What do you think you're doing, Daniel?" Mills snarled.

"Just finishing my Christmas shopping, sir. A few things for my first-grader," Daniel calmly replied.

"Have you forgotten this is one of the busiest days of our business?" Jack's voice grew louder, "Have you forgotten we're under a mandate to boost sales? Have you forgotten . . . ."

"Hold on!" Daniel interrupted. For once, he didn't care who was listening. "Mr. Mills, it's five fifty-eight. There are no customers in this department. In fact, I'd be willing to bet there are no more shoppers in the whole store. They've gone home to celebrate with their families. And that's what I'm going to do right now, if you'll excuse me."

"I will *not* excuse you, Watter," Jack Mills bellowed, "Meet me in my office as soon as you're through here." Daniel didn't see Jose follow him quietly to the manager's office.

(continued)

A NEW CHRISTMAS LEGEND (CONTINUED)

Daniel was well-liked and Jose was ready to come to the assistant's defense if necessary. Jose's holiday celebrations could wait for a few minutes. But it wasn't easy to eavesdrop on this conversation. Jose heard something that sounded like Jack Mills pounding his fist on a desk and a few accusations. Then he heard a quiet explanation, probably Watter, but Jose couldn't make the words out. There was another slamming noise—were they fighting? Jose wondered. After half an hour, he decided home for the holidays was better than fodder for office gossip. One worker, with no family to go home to, reported later that he saw Mills washing his face in the men's room about 8:00 P.M.

And this is where the story becomes legend. Most agree Jack Mills tried to fire Daniel Watter before the assistant manager quit. Others say Daniel, finally fed up, hit Mills in the face and gave him a bloody nose. Once, years later, a Sears employee walked up to Daniel and said, "Mr. Watter, you don't know me. But I once worked for Jack Mills and I have to shake your hand. Anyone that would hit Mills is a hero of mine."

"But I didn't hit him," Daniel smiled.

"You don't have to be modest with me, sir," the man said with a knowing look. And to this day, Daniel will tell you he didn't hit his boss. But what did happen to Mills was certainly a blow. When Chicago headquarters found out a store manager was trying to fire a young success story responsible for a 28 percent increase in sales, executives demoted Jack to a much smaller store. And they promoted Daniel to a cushy regional management job. He got Saturdays and evenings off. But he still doesn't buy Christmas gifts until December 24th. He says that's when you get the best deals.

~ LORRI V. ALLEN

Editor's note: Lorri Allen's father did work for a major retailer, and she did get a sewing machine and a Baby First Step once for Christmas. But that's where truth ends . . . or so she says. Lorri helps newsmakers get their stories across, www.soundbitecoach.com.

It may seem odd that a child would consider this a cherished present. But, when I received my first Bible at a tender age, I began to understand what Christmas represented. With all the hustle and bustle of the season (which now begins in July), I try to get quiet, cut out unnecessary craziness, and maintain a normalcy to focus on what matters. The simplicity allows me to truly savor the season.

~ LEE A. BARRON

In the old days, it was not called the holiday season; the Christians called it "Christmas" and went to church; the Jews called it "Hanukkah" and went to synagogue; the atheists went to parties and drank. People passing each other on the street would say "Merry Christmas!" or "Happy Hanukkah!" or (to the atheists) "Look out for the wall!"

~ DAVE BARRY
Christmas Shopping: A Survivor's Guide

When the hustle and bustle of the holiday season starts to feel overwhelming, I just love to sit on the couch with all the lights off, except for the glow of the fire in the fireplace and the glow of the lights on the Christmas tree. This experience always seems to leave the feeling of a warm, calm, happy glow inside me.

~ CONNIE JAMESON

CRYSTALLIZED MEMORIES

*S*erving and being served at the National Charity League's Annual Christmas Tea throughout high school gave me a sense of becoming a lady. Years later, I enjoyed a formal sit down Christmas Tea with my husband at the Ritz Carlton in Laguna Niguel, in Southern California, which overlooks the magnificent Pacific. A formal Christmas Tea should be enjoyed by everyone at least once.

Volunteerism was always valued in my family. One September I refurbished dolls, toys, bikes, wagons, etc. for Santa Claus Incorporated. Later in December, this fine organization invites you along with all its volunteers, to view your work on display before distributing these presents to needy families. As you walk into rooms full of toys, warmth cannot help but envelop your entire being, as you try to envision the child's face who might receive one of these treasures on Christmas morning.

"O Holy Night" had been beautifully sung by the soloist on the stage. I was singing during the A Capella Choir Christmas concert, from the school's auditorium balcony. I remember being donned in a choir robe and black velveteen pumps. Later, I walked past the football practice field, wearing a cute holiday dress. The college quarterback asked my brother "Who was that girl?"

Mom taught me how to decorate a Christmas tree. It always had a specific theme, and could give any department store window display a run for its money. She not only decorated the tree, but the front door, as well as the outside block wall which faced the street. One year in the 60s, we had a pink flocked tree with specks of silver mica, which she accentuated with clusters of silver ornaments. I think it was a noble fir, the kind with the big, full, beautiful branches.

(continued)

CRYSTALLIZED MEMORIES (CONTINUED)

Another year, she made a representation of a stained glass Madonna and Child to display on our front door. She rigged a light bulb inside the framed art, to give it effect. Before moving away from home, I went retro and decorated my mother's tree, with homemade gingerbread men and popcorn strung the old fashioned way. She decorated the door and the outside. It's a memory I still cherish as I decorate each year with my own whimsical themes.

We've all heard of a partridge in a pear tree, but have you ever heard of a hamster on a sleigh? Santa delivered one to my husband's workplace a few days before Christmas. We explained that Santa would not have room on his sleigh, let alone food or water on Christmas Eve. That is how we got Tonya, my daughter's first hamster. Little did we know that this first furry pet would start what I call the two turtledove effect. Five more hamsters followed the first, four guinea pigs (including one with a club foot—lest it be euthanized), six cats (several of which we adopted), a chameleon, a bird, and an abandoned tortoise named Dave.

~ LEE A. BARRON © COPYRIGHT 2007

CHRISTMAS CORNER
(How Christmas Becomes Young in December)

In a little corner of the year sits Christmas,
Waiting for us to notice her charms again.
Oh, "There you are! How great to see you!"
Christmas, our lost discovered friend!"

"Been so long.
You look marvelous darling!
Get fruitcakes to cook!
Get carols, let's sing!"

"Let's decorate for Christmas,
Our festive friend long lost.
Spare no holiday expense, elevate as we celebrate,
Whatever time or cost."

And they fall in love with Christmas,
So caught in her festive whirl.
That it's easy to forget,
Christmas is an old-fashioned kind of girl.

(continued)

(CONTINUED)

She does better with the slow dances,
Than ones so furious and fast.
She likes to breathe the Christmas air,
Before the moment's past.

Find the toasts, ring bells so proud,
Laud the praises on Christmas loud.
Drink with Christmas her merriment,
She takes to dance, before her time's spent.

As Christmas stands to take her dance,
The party says, "ho-hum."
Not appealing anymore,
The doomed dame, now done.

For Christmas knows as parties go,
To the next, the mad mob flurries.
"Give me action, quick holiday satisfaction,"
No time for Christmas worries.

Christmas, old Christmas,
Charming old gal plopped politely in the corner's bend.
Until the mob cycles round again,
From it's frenzy-loving trend.

(continued)

(CONTINUED)

And suddenly Christmas becomes,
Ever so beautiful and young.
They party and laugh and dance again,
More carols have been sung.

Christmas in your corner I see you,
Sitting so beautiful through that year.
You never tire of the folly de rol,
Of the Christmas atmosphere.

Christmas you beautiful giver,
That love filled corner of time.
Spread out through rooms of other days,
At least till Valentines'.

~ TERRI MARIE
© 2005

A USUAL,
EXTREMELY SPECIAL CHRISTMAS

*M*y most memorable Christmas has not yet come. It is only three days away. The usual Christmas Day at our house starts around seven o'clock in the morning. I wake up with Christmas wishes waiting to be fulfilled. The silence of the house makes me smile because only hours from this moment, the house will be full of hustle and bustle. I slowly walk down the dark hall toward our living room. The smell of cooking turkey fills the air and my mouth waters.

Thinking maybe my parents won't wake by themselves, I place the coffee pot on the stove and let it whistle awhile. Usually this does not work, so I quietly go into the living room and place the freshly made coffee at my parent's usual sitting spots. I stop for a moment and look at the tall full Christmas tree, decorated with all those heavy ornaments I used to make for my parents when I was very young. Then I notice the soft red stocking filled to the top with small presents just waiting to be opened. My hands want to rush and open all the presents but my heart says no.

By this time, Dad, an early riser, is awake and he wants me to wake Mom. Hesitating, I go to wake her but grab Mom's coffee thinking I will present the coffee as a peace offering for waking her so early. We gather in the living room and Dad puts on some Christmas music. He acts like Santa and joyfully gives out the presents. I can see the love and joy in his eyes as he watches Mom and me open our presents.

You see this may be a usual Christmas but it is very significant to me. About two months ago my father had a heart attack. I almost lost him forever. By the grace of God and Dad's will to live, this year we will be spending the usual, extremely special Christmas together.

~ ANNMARIE LARDIERI

THE "W" IN CHRISTMAS

*E*ach December, I vowed to make Christmas a calm and peaceful experience.

I had cut back on nonessential obligations—extensive card writing, endless baking, decorating, and even overspending. Yet still, I found myself exhausted, unable to appreciate the precious family moments, and of course, the true meaning of Christmas.

My son, Nicholas, was in kindergarten that year. It was an exciting season for a six year old. For weeks, he'd been memorizing songs for his school's "Winter Pageant." I didn't have the heart to tell him I'd be working the night of the production. Unwilling to miss his shining moment, I spoke with his teacher. She assured me there'd be a dress rehearsal the morning of the presentation. All parents unable to attend that evening were welcome to come then.

Fortunately, Nicholas seemed happy with the compromise. So, the morning of the dress rehearsal, I filed in ten minutes early, found a spot on the cafeteria floor and sat down. Around the room, I saw several other parents quietly scampering to their seats.

As I waited, the students were led into the room. Each class, accompanied by their teacher, sat cross-legged on the floor. Then, each group, one by one, rose to perform their song. Because the public school system had long stopped referring to the holiday as "Christmas," I didn't expect anything other than fun, commercial entertainment songs of reindeer, Santa Claus, snowflakes and good cheer.

So, when my son's class rose to sing, "Christmas Love," I was slightly taken aback by its bold title.

Nicholas was aglow, as were all of his classmates, adorned in fuzzy mittens, red sweaters, and bright snowcaps upon their heads.

(continued)

THE "W" IN CHRISTMAS (CONTINUED)

Those in the front row—center stage—held up large letters, one by one, to spell out the title of the song.

As the class would sing "C is for Christmas," a child would hold up the letter C. Then, "H is for Happy," and on and on, until each child holding up his portion had presented the complete message, "Christmas Love."

The performance was going smoothly, until suddenly, we noticed her; a small, quiet, girl in the front row holding the letter "M" upside down—totally unaware her letter "M" appeared as a "W." The audience of first through sixth graders snickered at this little one's mistake. But she had no idea they were laughing at her, so she stood tall, proudly holding her "W."

Although many teachers tried to shush the children, the laughter continued until the last letter was raised, and we all saw it together. A hush came over the audience and eyes began to widen.

In that instant, we understood the reason we were there, why we celebrated the holiday in the first place, why even in the chaos, there was a purpose for our festivities.

For when the last letter was held high, the message read loud and clear:

"C H R I S T W A S L O V E"

And, I believe, He still is.
Amazed in His presence . . . humbled by His love.

~ UNKNOWN

GOD'S CHRISTMAS PRESENT

Let me tell you the story,
Of the sweet Jesus Christ,
Who brought heaven to earth,
One cold winter night.

As planned by his Father,
A long time ago,
In the form of a babe,
He came down below.

His divine mission,
Unknown at the time,
Was later revealed,
When God felt inclined.

The day the sweet Lord,
Was nailed to that cross,
Was the day that God showed,
Mankind was not lost.

By the Son's grief and pain,
Man could be forgiven,
And God gave to man,
A vision of heaven.

But thick in his thinking,
And blind in his heart,
Man missed the Lord's meaning,
And remained in the dark.

Thus, each year at Christmas,
The tale is retold,
And man is reminded,
Of Jesus Christ's role.

Access to heaven,
God's gift to man,
God's Christmas present,
The start of His plan!

~ VIRGINIA (GINNY) ELLIS
www.poetrybyginny.com

THE ANGEL TREE

*S*haron was outraged. Several minutes passed as she waited behind a woman who was picking over the angels on the Christmas tree.

Every year the church collected names of needy children. Each one was represented by an angel on the Christmas tree in the foyer of the church. In the weeks proceeding Christmas, members of the congregation chose angels for whom they would buy gifts. Sharon had decided to join the church and she was feeling quite charitable. This would be her first act of kindness as a member. Who would God select for her to bless? As she neared the tree, she was dismayed to see a woman picking over the angels, rejecting one after another. "No, I don't want this one. It's a ten-year-old boy who wants sports equipment. I don't know a thing about sports." She pushed the angel aside and looked at another. "Here's a little girl who wants a dress. Forget it. Dresses are too expensive these days," the woman objected.

What kind of a giving spirit is that? Sharon thought. She clenched her teeth as she waited for the lady to make a decision and leave. Finally, the woman took an angel of her liking and exited.

I'm going to trust God to select the right angel for me, Sharon thought, with righteous indignation. In fact, I think I'll take two. She snatched two angels from the tree without reading them, shoved them in her pocket, and hurried away. She had never trusted God so sincerely before. She rushed to the car where her husband, Arnold, awaited. "Who is our Angel?" he asked.

"Actually, I took two. The lady in front of me was so selective on whom she was willing to buy for, I felt led to take two." She pulled the angels from her pocket.

(continued)

THE ANGEL TREE (CONTINUED)

"The first one is an eight-year-old boy who wants a football."

"Oh, that's easy." Arnold pulled the car into traffic thinking how simple this "giving thing" was going to be.

"The second one is . . ." Sharon gasped. "A dormitory of twenty-four fourteen-year-old girls!"

"Oh, my goodness," Arnold looked for a place to pull off the road. "Do you want to take it back and change it for another angel?"

Sharon was reminded of the indignation she felt when the other lady picked over the angels she didn't want. Hadn't Sharon trusted the Lord to give her the ones He selected especially for her?

"No, I couldn't. This is what God wants me to do."

In the following two weeks, Sharon gathered up 24 shoeboxes and took them to the school where she worked. She explained what they were for and invited all the staff to join in the fun of filling them with make-up, earrings, combs, mirrors, and all sorts of things fourteen-year-old girls would love. When the boxes were full, Sharon wrapped them in beautiful paper and took them to the church for delivery. When she walked away from the church, her spirit was multiplied twenty-five times.

There would be one eight-year-old boy and twenty-four fourteen-year-old girls who would receive Christmas gifts. But more important, Sharon, Arnold, and many others were blessed in their giving.

~ KAREN ROBERTSON
Speaker, author, coach, www.giantstepsuccess.com

LEE'S CHRISTMAS GIFT

*I*t was the first year of my marriage to Sharon and we had bought our first house together. Its gray stone façade surrounded us and helped us forge our new family unit. Her two sons, my stepsons, loved the house and the fact that they had their own playroom for their Lego's and other toys. It was also the third year of growing my new business, and times were tough. Cash flow was very tight.

One night, in early December, Sharon and I argued about money. We had savings but Sharon always looked on savings as sacred—not to be touched. During our argument, she yelled that we had no money and that we didn't even have the right dishes for the holidays. In the end, and reluctantly, she agreed we'd have to dip into savings. I had to promise to restore the "loan" as soon as business turned around.

What neither of us knew at the time was that Lee, her nine-year-old son, had heard at least part of our conversation. From what he heard, he came to believe that we were much worse off financially than we were and that we needed dishes.

The following weekend, Lee asked me to take him to do his Christmas shopping. When we arrived, he asked if I could take him to several of the stores, but wait for him outside, as he wanted his gifts to be a surprise. I smiled and readily agreed. We visited several stores and then he asked to go back to one of them. A few minutes later, he came out with a larger than expected box. It was carefully bagged to keep its contents a secret and he insisted on carrying it to the car and holding it on his lap all the way home.

That evening, he came down from his room and asked us for wrapping paper. Sharon offered to wrap for him, but he said he wanted to do it himself. It was a surprise, after all.

(continued)

LEE'S CHRISTMAS GIFT (CONTINUED)

The next day, I retrieved the paper, scissors, tape, and ribbon from his room. The package, wrapped lovingly as only a nine-year-old could, sat in the corner. Lee was off somewhere playing and returning incidentals like wrapping paper just didn't occur to him.

I called Sharon to the room to show her the present. We looked at each other and asked, "What can it be?" We also wondered if there were other presents we hadn't seen, as Lee had only a small budget. We closed the bedroom door, leaving the present in its place of honor.

Christmas morning, both Adam (her eldest) and Lee were awake and downstairs at the break of dawn. Consciously, as only boys can, they generated enough noise to wake us beyond any chance of rolling over. We joined them. The tree was beautiful with almost two dozen gifts spread beneath its boughs. A unanimous decision placed gift opening before breakfast. I started the distribution and we began to open our gifts. After two toys each for the boys, Lee asked if we could open his present next. He told us he had spoken to Adam about giving him a gift and they had decided that a gift that the family really needed was more important. Sharon and I looked at each other, curiosities ablaze. "What was this present?" Lee waited proudly with Adam smiling at his side. We opened the package.

It was a set of Melamine dishes: four plates, four cups, four saucers, four bowls, four salad dishes. We looked at each other, perplexed. We did not recall the argument. But we were both good at fast recoveries. Hugs, kisses, and grateful thanks followed. Sharon told Lee he shouldn't have spent so much (for him) just for us. It was then that he told us he had heard us arguing and hoped that his $15 would be enough to help us in our time of need.

(continued)

LEE'S CHRISTMAS GIFT (CONTINUED)

I will never forget that moment. Tears were just the edge of it. How do you adequately thank someone for such a gift? These days, Lee teaches and is happily married. Adam is doing well. Sharon has her life in England. I am surrounded by friends and still have my business, nearly 30 years later; I have been blessed. Each holiday season I think of Lee's gift, and always will.

~ JOHN REDDISH

And in the sixth month the angel Gabriel was sent from God unto a city of Galilee, named Nazareth, to a virgin espoused to a man whose name was Joseph, of the house of David; and the virgin's name was Mary. And the angel came in unto her, and said, "Hail, thou that art highly favoured, the Lord is with thee: blessed art thou among women." And when she saw him, she was troubled at his saying, and cast in her mind what manner of salutation this should be. And the angel said unto her, "Fear not, Mary: for thou hast found favour with God. And, behold, thou shalt conceive in thy womb, and bring forth a son, and shalt call his name Jesus."

~ LUKE 1:26-31

CHRISTMAS TOYS

Children staring through the window,
Fingers pointing to displays,
Noses pressed against the glass,
Ooh's and ahh's and yeah's and hey's.

Toys now, the likes of which,
Older folks cannot perceive,
Far beyond their comprehension,
They're amazed and so naive.

Computer things for savvy teens,
Robotic toys for tots,
Animals that bounce and pounce,
Push their tummies and they walk.

Expensive electronic toys,
On each wish list this year,
Desktops, laptops, hand held devices,
Every kid's an engineer.

Technical, optical, digital,
Printers, and keyboards, and mice,
Cordless, wireless, portable,
Hah! Won't this Christmas be nice!

(continued)

(CONTINUED)

Megabytes, gigabytes, megahertz,
The more, the merrier, it seems,
The bigger, the broader, the wider,
The better, those monitor screens.

Hardware, software, disks that save,
And drives that burn CDs,
Machines that copy, scan, and print,
And drives for DVDs.

A little girl stood at the window,
Gazing at everything with awe,
"Mama," she said and pointed,
"That's what I want . . . that doll."

Propped atop a Christmas box,
High upon a plastic shelf,
Totally out of place, it seemed,
Sat a doll, all by itself.

"But, honey," her mother smiled and said,
"I doubt that dolly can talk,
She's not electronically endowed,
So she cannot creep nor walk."

(continued)

(CONTINUED)

"I don't care," said the little girl,
"I just want her to hold and hug,
Like mamas do for babies,
When they want to show them love."

"I want to hold her in my arms,
And rock her fast asleep,
She doesn't have to talk or walk,
Or need to cry or creep."

And so the mother bought the doll,
For her wise and precious child,
"I guess new things aren't always best,"
She decided then, and smiled.

Far better to hold a baby doll,
Than to hold a remote control,
Far better to know of hugs and love,
Than of things electronic and cold.

~ VIRGINIA (GINNY) ELLIS
© December 2006
www.poetrybyginny.com

RELAX, IT'S DECEMBER

A friend recently wrote, "Relax during the holidays. Enjoy this wonderful time." Ha! Easy for him to say.

How can we relax when there is so much to do? We have to plan, shop for gifts, buy the gifts, buy the bows, wrap the gifts, deliver the gifts, find cards, address cards, buy stamps, stamp and mail the cards, bake, clean, shop for food, put up a tree, decorate the tree, cook, clean some more, find the lights, hang them outside, be cheerful, find something to wear to the parties, attend parties, write thank-you notes, pack, buy the plane ticket, and donate to charities.

I don't think Mary had it much easier. Can you imagine being nine months pregnant and traveling seventy miles on a donkey? She, of all people, may have been able to relax. But I can imagine her thinking, "No room at the inn, after that trip? All I wanted was a soft bed and a hot bath. That donkey ride was a great way to get the baby to arrive a few days early. Now, I need bed clothes, baby clothes, baby wipes, bottles, pacifiers, diapers, announcement cards—not everyone heard the angels—thank-you notes (even for those strange gifts from the foreigners—did they leave an address?), and air freshener—those cows, phew."

Poor Mary. When the angel told her she was having God's son, she might have imagined it would be easy, if not glamorous. Maybe her experience is why some of us are hard-wired to make December challenging. We will not deliver the son of God, but we can kill ourselves trying to deliver presents designed to celebrate his birth.

Our expectations of ourselves run so high this season. We have memories to live up to. Or we are desperately trying to create new memories to erase ones that have never lived up to the hype.

(continued)

RELAX, IT'S DECEMBER (CONTINUED)

Some of us, brought up in traditions that saw Christmas as just another day to celebrate the birth, death, and resurrection of Jesus, may have had it right: the mere fact that God came as a helpless baby to an apathetic world is a reason to celebrate all the time, not just in December.

My friend who can relax may have a point. The shepherds visited, the Magi gave and the angels sang. So maybe we do not have to do it all. Fortunately, there are many ways to share the joy that a baby born in a barn made it possible for us to live in mansions for eternity.

Whatever your strategy for marking Jesus' earthly arrival, may you live your life changed by his love.

~ LORRI V. ALLEN
Speaker, author, reporter, www.lorri.com

After returning from a shopping trip with her father, my then four-year-old daughter, Amy, exclaimed, "Whatever we got you Mommy we didn't get you scissors!"

~ LEE A. BARRON

OH CHRISTMAS TREE

Twinkle, twinkle little star
she sat on the curb right next to the car
like a January Christmas tree
wearing garish jewelry

a left hand star atop her hand
a well worn ornamental band
a rosy lip
a frosted head

a smile—very close to dead
drooping shoulders
sagging branches
a magnet for nostalgic glances

shining brightly
glittering nightly
each spare pound was wrapped up tightly
worn out second hand Christmas tree
—it looks way too much like me!

~ JACQUELINE MOSES

THE MOST BEAUTIFUL TREE

Its trunk was straight
(a wooden pole stolen from a real tree)
and went down the middle in pull-apart sections,
it had holes drilled all around
like woodpecker's marks
where our young and eager hands
would fit in the "branches"—
these were made of silver foil
like magic eyelashes fluttering in twisted rows
round the thin wire strands
and ending
at the tips
in a spray-burst glittering silver "flower"
unlike any a forest tree had ever grown.

We twisted and crammed the silver wire branches
into the pre-drilled holes each year
and each year they grew a bit more limp and dull
without our gleeful notice.

We untangled the heavy strings of colored lights
the strands which had such ancient bulbs
they were no longer replaceable
and burnt our tender fingertips upon curious touch.

(continued)

THE MOST BEAUTIFUL TREE (CONTINUED)
My father would set up the base which
had a rotating light show going on beneath
where blue, red, green took turns
making the metallic silver branches glow like heaven
and the now and then placed "bubble lights" he screwed
into the regular light strands at random spots
fairly stole the show
percolating away happily with a cheery sound and rhythm
similar to our father's laugh as he watched us
digging out our favorites from the wrapped decorations.

Clipped into the branches
were our 1950's era blown-glass "birds"
with springy "tails" of bobbing tinsel.
We watched the finished tree,
mesmerized by the psychedelic colors and movement
long light years it seemed
from my coming days of hippie glee.

Those days were the innocent
those Christmases were the treasured and rare
our home life—both sublime and unfamiliar
in those few years we took that tinsel tree
from attic to living room
from discombobulated bright glittering hope
to tarnishing and rumpled and forgotten
magic-less heap.

(continued)

THE MOST BEAUTIFUL TREE (CONTINUED)
Fifty-something years later
in a cluttered thrift store
I run across a dirty cardboard box
and though it is fairly smashed and buried beneath
the twisted discards of strangers
I recognize at once the faded once-bright print
and the illustration of the rotating tri-colored light.

I pass by the dingy box
and manage not to peak inside
or disturb its retired splendor.

I head out the store's door and a bell rings as I do
and for a very brief moment
I hear jingle bells and my father's laughter
bouncing off the most beautiful tree
I have ever seen—
the silver tree with bright bubbles and glass birds
of my sometimes magical youth
and instantly know
why to this day
I can't resist glittery sparkly things
—it's an ode to childhood's tree of dreams.

~ RETA TAYLOR
© 2007 Reta Lorraine Bowen Taylor

365 DAYS OF SPARKLE

Believing strongly that the true essence of Christmas is not only on one day every year, my white spiral lighted Christmas tree is up all year long, in my TV room, donned with cherished ornaments of great sentimental value from my travels and dearest of friends. Christmas lives on for me—every day! Whenever I pass by it, any day of the year, I remember that friend and the heartfelt love we share. And yes, having the tree up all year through does let the cat play with the lower ornaments for more than the typically designated two-week period . . . so he's a happy kitty, too! Loving the sparkle, I also keep up metallic garlands of different colors around the house all year long. It brings joy to my heart. At Thanksgiving the garland is gold, orange, olive green with beautifully color-coordinated autumn leaves. Then there's purple and bright yellow for Easter. And silver and gold stars throughout the year. One of my friends asked me once, "Do you think that you can ever have too much sparkle?" "I don't think so!" I think the world could use more sparkle—what better way to see hope, joy, optimism, and feel good about yourself even in dull times.

~ SHERYL ROUSH

A REAL-LIFE SCROOGE

I find it ironic that at the age of forty it was my three boys, David Brett (ten), Jordan Scott (seven), and Isaac Jake (five), who taught me the holiday lesson. I don't know the origin of my belief but I always felt that holidays were a hassle. My cynical view included the thoughts that family obligations and social expectations drove the actions of many and that authentic meaningful celebratory activities were few and far between. The commercial nature of the holidays added to my disenchantment. My wife accurately referred to me as a real life "Scrooge."

Thankfully my kids had my wife, and I had my kids. Being of the Jewish faith, my wife put tremendous effort into making Hannukah a joyful holiday for our boys. With our Hannukah celebration behind us you can imagine my surprise when I came home from running errands on Christmas Eve and found three socks hung on the mantle of our fireplace. Now these were not ordinary red and white decorated Christmas socks; these were miniature stained white athletic tube socks with the name of each one of our boys illegibly scribbled.

I, Mr. Scrooge himself, chuckled and cracked a small smile. My youngest child, Isaac, was quick to provide me an explanation. "Daddy, Santa Claus doesn't care if we don't celebrate Christmas. Mommy told us he would stop by and put candy in our socks if we hung them up." Who was I to argue?

Extremely early that Christmas morning, I awoke to the thumps of Isaac tapping on my shoulder. He noticed I hadn't hung a sock and felt sad because Santa didn't leave me any candy. He told me not to worry and offered to share his candy canes with me.

(continued)

A REAL-LIFE SCROOGE (CONTINUED)

I basked in the glory of his selfless act of sharing as we spoke of giving to those less fortunate than ourselves. In this case, his own daddy.

He gave me more than candy canes though. His actions triggered a change in my attitude. Holidays are rich with learning opportunities and I need to stow away my Scrooge attitude for good. I now look forward to the next holiday and the learning opportunity it presents for me.

~ MICHAEL BRUCE

DON WE NOW OUR GAY APPAREL

A little girl was watching her parents dress for a party. When she saw her dad donning his tuxedo, she warned, "Daddy, you shouldn't wear that suit." "And why not, darling?" "You know that it always gives you a headache the next morning."

~ UNKNOWN

DOLLS AND STROLLERS

At Christmas, we gave our one and a half year old Faith a doll. She proudly put it in the stroller she'd also just opened. Then a little bit later a relative gave her a doll and when she opened it, she promptly pulled the other doll out and threw it to the ground, placing the "new" doll into the stroller. A little later, doll number three was opened and she repeated the process—threw down doll number two onto the floor and put the "new" one in the stroller. Moral of the story—perhaps one doll at a time is best! (And as for triplets or the third child . . . you decide—does anyone get pushed aside?)

~ JENNIFER ROUSSEAU SEDLOCK
www.jenniferspeaks.com

MEALS ON WHEELS

While working for an organization that delivers lunches to elderly shut-ins, I used to take my four-year-old daughter on my afternoon rounds during the holidays. She was unfailingly intrigued by the various appliances of old age, particularly the canes, walkers, and wheelchairs. One day I found her staring at a pair of false teeth soaking in a glass. As I braced myself for the inevitable barrage of questions, she merely turned and whispered, "The tooth fairy will never believe this!"

~ UNKNOWN

DO YOU BELIEVE?

The family attended Christmas Eve service together, bringing my nephew Peter, and niece Alison, to their first Christian services, since moving from Australia to the United States. When the minister invited the small children forward to hear the story of the birth of Christ, little three-year-old Alison went to the front of the pulpit and attentively listened. Back to the pews, we stood and sang numerous hymns, followed by the outdoor candle lighting service and more songs. Driving back to my parents house in a quiet moment Alison broke the silence with her precious Aussie dialect, "Auntie Sheryl, do you believe in Jesus?"

"Yes I do."

With self-assuredness she replied, "I thought so!" (I silently gasped for air to keep myself from crying deeply at this momentous occasion.)

~ SHERYL ROUSH

Love is what's in the room with you at Christmas if you stop opening presents and listen.

~ UNKNOWN, ATTRIBUTED TO A SEVEN-YEAR-OLD NAMED BOBBY

NEW PANTS

Many years ago, I was unable to return home for Christmas and spent the holiday at the home of a friend. This wonderful family included three-year-old James who had just received a new pair of pants from Santa. Santa was aware that James was known for tearing the pockets out of his pants because this new pair of pants were "pocket-free."

I watched with amusement as he kept trying to push his fists into the smooth seams on the side of his pants. Finally in desperation, he looked up at me and said, "Amy, I ain't got no pockets!"

"James," I corrected his grammar, "I don't have *any* pockets."

He thought about this for a minute and then replied, "I don't either!"

~ AMY COLLINS
www.thecadencegrp.com

READING THE FAMILY BIBLE

A little boy opened the big family Bible. He was fascinated as he fingered through the old pages. Suddenly, something fell out of the Bible. He picked up the object and looked at it. What he saw was an old leaf that had been pressed in between the pages.

"Mama, look what I found," the boy called out.

"What have you got there, dear?"

With astonishment in the young boy's voice, he answered, "I think it's Adam's underwear."

~ UNKNOWN

THE GIFT OF MAGIC

*M*agic happened regularly around our house when I was a child. My family has always celebrated everything. Because our farm was somewhat isolated, the family traditions that our parents created were the mainstay of my childhood.

As in most households, Thanksgiving, Christmas, and Easter were eagerly anticipated festivities, but we had additional holidays. One of those celebrations was "Three Wise Kings." My mom said it was because we were Swiss-Italian and lived in the country, making it easy for the Three Wise Kings to park their camels outside our house. (Three Wise Kings is also known as Twelfth Night, celebrated twelve days after Christmas on January 6. It honors the Magi who followed the Star of Bethlehem, bringing gold, frankincense, and myrrh to the infant Jesus.)

Because the Three Wise Kings had to travel so far on camelback, they could only bring us small gifts—usually an orange or tangerine, an apple, sometimes an avocado or mango, plus a small sweet and about twenty-five cents in coins. We loved Three Wise Kings Day because it made us feel special.

My parents went all out to create magic in our lives. One year, my mom excused herself during dinner. Suddenly, through the window, we saw a camel. (She had acquired a huge stuffed camel and was outside, moving it up and down.) We shrieked with excitement and awe, knowing the Kings were passing by. The next morning, we awoke to find jewels strung everywhere on the bushes and vines. There were camels' hoof prints and camel dung and a note that this had been a great year for the Magi, so they were sharing their wealth.

(continued)

THE GIFT OF MAGIC (CONTINUED)

I vividly remember the sensation of utter delight and can still see the shimmering jewels hanging from the trees. My parents had created the illusion with used costume jewelry from a Goodwill store, horse-made hoof prints, and horse manure posing as camel dung. To this day, the nuns who taught us at school recall our wide-eyed awe when we retold the tale and how completely we believed.

At Christmas, we didn't always get something we had asked for. Of course, we'd be disappointed. Later in the day, Dad would suggest we take a Jeep ride around the ranch to see if anything had fallen off the sleigh. Sure enough! Down at a barn or dangling in a grapevine would be that special gift. Once, a bicycle was sticking out of the chimney with a note attached: "Sorry, it wouldn't squeeze down."

Every holiday provided an opportunity for my parents to be creative. We saw the Easter Bunny, we felt the Tooth Fairy's kiss. We witnessed Santa and his elves flying through the sky with Rudolph's red light leading the reindeer. My sister Debbie remained an avid believer well into her teens. Eventually, my parents had to tell her that it was all "magic."

As we grew and questions arose, their response was, "If you don't believe in magic, magic never happens." I decided to believe. Today, my children delight at the magic they experience year-round in our household. The Three Wise Kings still visit, although my kids are only half Swiss-Italian.

In an un-magical world, you create the magic in your life. Find ways to reinterpret your daily routine through the eyes of a child. Children give us a second chance to view the world with innocence and credulity.

(continued)

THE GIFT OF MAGIC (CONTINUED)

What magic is hiding in your soul?

What simple things can become magical experiences if you use a little imagination?

Exercise: Be Your Own Fairy Godmother

Imagine that you are a magician with a magic wand. You can even make a wand from a stick. Add a few ribbons or a sparkling star, and presto! You hold the key to power. Wave the magic wand over your head when you want to change something, even your mood. The magic to create the life you want is inside you. Dream it. Do it.

If you don't make magic, magic doesn't happen.

Have happy, healthy, and holy holiday seasons!

~ CYNTHIA BRIAN

Speaker, author

"The Gift of Magic" is excerpted by Cynthia Brian's award winning book, Be the Star You Are

© *2001-2007 Cynthia Brian*

www.star-style.com

www.bethestaryouare.org

THE LITTLE BROWN BULB

In a little old factory way up on a hill,
Is a lot of machinery which sounds loud and shrill.
It bumps, pumps, binks, and klinks.
Half of it goes up and the other half sinks.
The man who invented it stands on a lever.
He pulls, then pushes. One can see he is clever.
In falls the glass, the paint, and the tin.
It's all ground up in a great big bin.

At the front of the machine is a tiny door,
and from it falls Christmas tree bulbs onto the floor.
They bounce and they roll and for goodness sake,
when they knock together, some of them break.
As the inventor watches it makes him sad.
But, if the brown ones break it makes him glad.
He likes only the blue, the green, the red, and the gold.
If the brown ones don't break, they never get sold.

One day a little brown bulb slipped under a broom.
He knew that if he was seen, it would be his doom.
At the end of the day he was quiet as a fox.
The broom was moved and he slid into a box.
Next to a blue one he felt comfortable and bold.
If no one discovered him, he'd probably be sold!
One day later he was in a store on a shelf,
Having bad dreams that he was all by himself.

(continued)

THE LITTLE BROWN BULB (CONTINUED)

When he felt the box move, he giggled with joy.
By the sound of the voice . . . he was picked up by a boy!
In his new home he could smell the pine.
To be perched on a branch would be just fine.
When the box was opened he saw the boy frown,
And yell, "I got gypped" . . . "One of these is brown."
He lay all-alone on the floor by a chair.
He'd never see Christmas like the bulbs up there.

I'll be stepped on and swept up with old tinsel, you see.
No toys, boys, joys . . . Oh gee!
When all of a sudden the mother reached down,
"I've just the spot for this bulb that is brown."
She carried him to the crib where Jesus lay,
Screwed him into the socket and knelt to pray.
His light brightened up the stable inside.
He was so filled with joy he could have cried.

He knew about Christmas in Bethlehem town,
'Cause he was the bulb that turned out to be brown.

~ DANIEL H. JAMES (FATHER), AND
MARK S. JAMES (SON), 8 YEARS OLD
DECEMBER 16, 1963
© 1963

Christmas is forever,
Not for just one day.
For loving, sharing, giving,
Are not to put away.
Like bells and lights and tinsel,
in some box upon a shelf.

The good you do for others,
Is good you do yourself.

~ NORMAN W. BROOKS
"Let Every Day Be Christmas"

Yes, Virginia, there is a Santa Claus. He exists as certainly as love and generosity and devotion exists, and you know that they abound and give to your life its highest beauty and joy.

~ CHARLES DANA
Editorial in the New York Sun, *1897, responding to a letter from eight-year-old Virginia O'Hanlon*

It was always said of him, that he knew how to keep Christmas well, if any man alive possessed the knowledge. May that be truly said of us, and all of us! And so, as Tiny Tim observed, "God bless us, every one!"

~ CHARLES DICKENS

Christmas is a time when you get homesick—even when you're home.

~ CAROL NELSON

We hear the beating of wings over Bethlehem and a light that is not of the sun or of the stars shines in the midnight sky. Let the beauty of the story take away all narrowness, all thought of formal creeds. Let it be remembered as a story that has happened again and again, to men of many different races, that has been expressed through many religions, that has been called by many different names. Time and space and language lay no limitations upon human brotherhood.

~ THE NEW YORK TIMES, 25 DECEMBER 1937
Quoted in Quotations for Special Occasions *by Maud van Buren, 1938*

Only in souls the Christ is brought to birth,
And there he lives and dies.

~ ALFRED NOYES

Christmas waves a magic wand over this world, and behold, everything is softer and more beautiful.

~ NORMAN VINCENT PEALE

Christmas is the day that holds all time together.

~ ALEXANDER SMITH

Christmas renews our youth by stirring our wonder. The capacity for wonder has been called our most pregnant human faculty, for in it are born our art, our science, our religion.

~ RALPH SOCKMAN

For centuries men have kept an appointment with Christmas. Christmas means fellowship, feasting, giving, and receiving, a time of good cheer, home.

~ W.J. RONALD TUCKER

Wouldn't life be worth the living
Wouldn't dreams be coming true
If we kept the Christmas spirit
All the whole year through?

~ UNKNOWN

There's more, much more, to Christmas than candlelight and cheer;
It's the spirit of sweet friendship that brightens all year.
It's thoughtfulness and kindness, it's hope reborn again,
For peace, for understanding, And for goodwill to men!

~ UNKNOWN

WHERE ARE THE LIGHTS?

The tradition in our family is to take a drive and look at Christmas lights around town. I have done this every year with my son, Steven, since he was a little guy; he is now eighteen years old. A couple of years ago we decided that it was time to bring my two-year-old niece, Emily, into the tradition. When picked her up from her parents', she was bundled up in her holiday pajamas and was ready to go. As soon as she saw a stream of lights she screamed, "There is the lights, there they are!" We were on our way to the local racetrack known for their amazing light displays, about a thirty minute car ride. It was thirty minutes of, "Where did the lights go, Auntie? Where are the lights? Where did the lights go?" My son and I were cracking up.

The following year we picked her up, and to our amazement, she remembered everything from the prior year ... "Where are the lights, Auntie?" I loved it and I look forward to many years of this tradition.

~ STEPHANIE CRISE

GRANDMA'S PANTRY

We drove cross-country in the old station wagon to see our relatives, driving from sunny San Diego to "cold country": Iowa, Nebraska, and Minnesota. Our reward—being met by Grandma Nellie with a freshly baked assortment of cookies in the walk-in pantry: ginger snaps, pfeffernuesse cookies (a German delight made with strong pepper nuts and clove), and snicker doodles (cinnamon and sugar cookies). In the cold mornings, after milking the cows and feeding the pigs, she would make deep-fried rosettes—donut-like pastries, dipped in powdered sugar. There was never a leftover!

~ SHERYL ROUSH

HOME AND HOPE AT THE HOLIDAYS

*H*olidays are customs we've come to observe over the generations. Meant to be festive, one of the many ways we observe holiday festivities is to be with family and friends. Where our family is, usually we want to be for the holidays. Many of us have packed up the car and traveled far to be with family.

I remember as a kid when nine of us crammed into an old Terraplane to travel to see relatives over the Christmas vacation. The Terraplane was a car brand and model built by the Hudson Motor Car Company of Detroit, Michigan, between 1932 and 1939. It was not a large car. Seven kids, ages six to eighteen, and mom and dad, had to pack in like sardines to fit. Good thing buckling up with seat belts wasn't required then. To save space, we packed only two changes of clothes each for the week's stay. Restrooms and restaurants were far apart. We ate packed lunches and found private places in the woods for bathroom breaks. The drive took us through five states from Michigan to Mississippi. It was the first time to go back since we moved to Michigan from a small farm town in Mississippi four years earlier.

We were to start our Christmas vacation trip after the last day of school. The trip got off to a rocky start for me. Once all of us were in the car and on the road, far enough away from home and on strange territory, my older sister pulled out my diary. She read from my diary in the car for everyone to hear about how I'd stayed after school and played "spin the bottle" at a classmate's house party. I guess that's what brothers and sisters do to one another. Even so, we were united as a family, traveling far to be in Jackson, the big city, with gramma, aunts, uncles, and cousins.

(continued)

HOME AND HOPE AT THE HOLIDAYS (continued)

One of the most fun things we did all the way to Mississippi was look for the Burma-Shave signs. Each phrase was on a separate sign, and there were usually five signs total, all miles apart. We read one sign, and anxiously watched to catch the sight of another one. Miles would go by. With only a few words as a clue each time, we were kept in suspense. Corny as they were, they kept us curious for hours. Here is one of the slogans we might have read back in the fifties:

"To Kiss"... (miles later)... "a mug"... (miles later)... "that's like a cactus"... (miles later)... "takes more nerve"... (miles later)... "Than it does practice"... (miles later)... "Burma-Shave"

It was a long trip and trying at times. But as kids, it was such an adventure. Even though there were nine of us, hungry and tired when we arrived in Mississippi, we were warmly welcomed by Aunt Loney, Uncle Desmond, and Gramma. Their two-bedroom home was crowded, but they would never turn us away for lack of room. It was good to renew memories and satisfy taste buds with the southern hospitality of my heritage. I enjoyed greasy beans, black-eyed peas, grits, fried okra, and fried chicken. Family favorite foods and familiarity gave us great comfort. Most importantly, we were together as a family again. Two years later our father was no longer with us to drive that old Terraplane to visit relatives at Christmastime.

Most recently, my Christmastime ritual became flying to Baltimore to celebrate with my daughter, Kristen and her family. On Christmas Eve we go to church together, with the kids usually taking part in the service. Home fairly early, we share the ritual of gift wrapping, and filling stockings. Then in the wee hours, once the kids are in bed and fast asleep, we play Santa. As family, we have rituals we've developed, and we find great pleasure and comfort in sharing them.

(continued)

HOME AND HOPE AT THE HOLIDAYS (CONTINUED)

On Christmas morning, with cinnamon rolls in front of us, we open stockings and gifts leisurely. Then we finish packing the van and head for Michigan where we meet up with my other daughter, Lisa and her family. It's worth the long trip, packing the van to the hilt with more gifts for them. The trip is sometimes made longer because of rain and snow and diaper changes. We're glad to do it to be with daughters and grandkids, sisters and brothers, nieces and nephews, and cousins. We have gifts to exchange, food to share, and time to be together as family, creating memories.

We're all familiar with car trips taken in order to be home for the holidays—upsets and conflicts; full bladders and empty stomachs; boredom and sleepiness. No matter what family argument, or disagreements, or unkind words transpire, we're usually willing to put those aside and realize how lucky we are to have one another.

However, holidays can be a sad time for some. Holidays don't always meet our expectations. Even in the midst of family, sometimes holidays make us feel more alone. Some don't have family to share with. Others don't have that special someone to remember him or her with a gift. Some of us have memories of tragic events in our life at Christmastime. There may have been a death, sickness, depression, unemployment, or alienation from family.

No matter how alone we may feel at this time of year, we can reach out to others who might include us in their holiday plans, or who we need to include in ours. We can start our own "family" and traditions. We can remember that Christmas is the very event that gives us hope, and helps us overcome a feeling of emptiness.

~ EMMA LAVONNE

Weave in faith and God will find the thread.

~ PROVERB

Christmas is for children. But it is for grownups too. Even if it is a headache, a chore, and nightmare, it is a period of necessary defrosting of chill and hide-bound hearts.

~ LENORA MATTINGLY WEBER

When Christmas bells are swinging above the fields of snow, we hear sweet voices ringing from lands of long ago, and etched on vacant places are half-forgotten faces of friends we used to cherish, and loves we used to know.

~ ELLA WHEELER WILCOX
Christmas Fancies Poems of Power

Our hearts grow tender with childhood memories and love of kindred, and we are better throughout the year for having, in spirit, become a child again at Christmas-time.

~ LAURA INGALLS WILDER

MY ONLY WHITE CHRISTMAS

One Christmas Eve I left the sunshine of Southern California for the wilds of Washington State to visit my oldest brother T.P. and his wife Marie.

As the plane descended into Seattle, I saw nothing but clouds. Good, I thought, we will have a white Christmas. Due to these same clouds, the little puddle jumper that would take me over the Cascade Mountains into Wenatchee could not fly that night. Instead, we piled onto a bus for the four-hour ride over the mountains. My fellow bus mates and I grumbled about being on a bus Christmas Eve, missing dinner, the inconvenience to our families, etc. We were a pitiful lot feeling very sorry for ourselves.

As midnight neared, a clear voice in the back of the bus started singing "Silent Night." Pretty soon we all were singing, crying, and laughing. When we finally pulled into the Wenatchee Airport I thought T.P. had forgotten me but no, around the corner he came. He had the foresight to call the airport ahead of time before making the long drive to get me.

On the way up the road it started to snow, well at least it "spit" as T.P. would say. It never really snowed that Christmas although it tried. I look back fondly at that Christmas I spent with my brother. A few years later MS would ravage his body and ultimately cost him his life. That was my one and only "White Christmas."

~ BECKY PALMER

WAKE UP AND SMELL THE PINECONES

The Christmas celebration I remember the best was when my family was poorest.

It was Christmas 1977. I was sixteen years old. My dad had given up his well-paying management job in Washington, DC, and moved the family to Chattanooga so he could go back to school. My mother worked full-time as a kindergarten teacher, and Dad threw an early morning paper route to help make ends meet. Adjusting to these changes in our lives was not easy for my eleven-year-old sister and me.

Several weeks before Christmas, I overheard Mom telling Dad she was worried about how she was going to buy gifts for us, but beautifully wrapped packages soon piled up under the tree.

When Christmas morning arrived, I flew down the stairs and ripped open the presents. Then, I dumped out my red flannel stocking with my name embroidered on it. In seconds, my holiday excitement turned to disappointment—with a capital "D." The boxes were filled with used clothes from a nearby thrift store, and my stocking was stuffed with oranges, candy canes, and a toothbrush. To make matters worse, I had to spend the day with people I did not even know. Mom had invited some people from church who didn't have anywhere to go to join us for the holiday.

I tried not to look as disappointed as I felt, but Mom knew. She knelt down and gave my sister and me a big hug. She smiled and said, "I'm sorry we don't have many gifts this year, but think about how fortunate we are. We have a family, we are all healthy, and we have the opportunity to show hospitality to people who need it."

(continued)

WAKE UP AND SMELL THE PINECONES (CONTINUED)

Fortunate? I didn't think so. In fact, I was embarrassed. What was I going to tell my friends? The first question everyone would ask is "What did you get for Christmas?" It took me years to realize and finally admit it, but this was my favorite and most memorable Christmas.

- *I learned I could enjoy Christmas no matter what my circumstances, and I know it's okay to feel sad or disappointed. Sharing those feelings can be important, especially if you have experienced a loss.*
- *I take time to reflect on what the season really means to me and decide how I can incorporate my values in my holiday plans and set priorities.*
- *I set limits on my spending and don't feel the need to impress anyone with how much I give or get.*
- *I've learned that joy comes from giving to others, and I know that time can be the most valuable gift of all.*
- *I try to keep an "attitude of gratitude" all year long with a "Grateful List" I add to daily. Before you can open a present at my house, you have to tell something you are grateful for.*

It was because of that Christmas many years ago that I woke up, smelled the pinecones, and realized how important relationships are. Christmas is a wonderful time for creating memories. Wherever you are, be there!

~ KATHY B. DEMPSEY

VEGAN CHRISTMAS

'Twas the night before Christmas, and all through the house,
Nothing's overnight baking, not lamb and not grouse.
Making plans for the morning, health-conscious are we,
Jotting it down, while sipping white green tea.
We'll start with wheatgrass—a two-ounce shot,
Toasting healthy bodies with no meat in the pot.
Most thankful are we as we pause to say grace,
For not getting caught up in the holiday rat race.
Sparkling pomegranate juice in a wine glass,
Light up the stove—we're cookin' with gas!
Pita chips and hummus are starter pre-meal,
Carrots, jicama, bell peppers—the natural deal.
Uncork the vintage sauvignon blanc,
Segura Viudas Spanish bubbly you can take to the bank!
Fresh garden salad, sunflower seeds, and sprouts,
There's enough for everyone—so no one pouts.
Simmer a pot of couscous, or basmati rice,
Baked butternut squash would surely be nice.
Raw sugar snap peas, and baked yummy yam,
Doing well avoiding duck, turkey, and ham.
Brown rice bread, lentil veggie soup, too.
Wow—without meat and dairy—there's so much you can do!
Chocolate tofu mousse cake—well-chilled,
With graham cracker crust, I'm not that strong-willed!
Organic pumpkin pie—served piping hot.
Sugar-free, you ask? I think *not*!

~ SHERYL ROUSH
www.sparklepresentations.com

IT'S TIME FOR A HOLIDAY
As the cold months come near
Snow blanketing the earth
The animals have no fear
Instincts form from birth
For they know what they must do
They have done it all along
It's almost time to start a new
To bring spring in with a cheerful song
But before that can happen
They must close their little eyes
And start nappin'
But for us humans it's another story
We have our own plan in mind
Time to stock up your inventory
Don't be blind
It's time for a holiday!
There's different ones for every culture
Everyone say "Hooray!"
Family members come from a far
To help you celebrate
So jump into the car
And don't be late
There's lots of yummy food and drinks
Gifts and presents too
But when it's over, that just stinks!

~ SHENAY KLOSS, AGE 13

Christmas, my child, is love in action. Every time we love, every time we give, it's Christmas.

~ DALE EVANS ROGERS

Love came down at Christmas; love all lovely, love divine;
love was born at Christmas, stars and angels gave the sign.

~ CHRISTINA G. ROSSETTI

Christmas—that magic blanket that wraps itself about us, that something so intangible that it is like a fragrance. It may weave a spell of nostalgia. Christmas may be a day of feasting, or of prayer, but always it will be a day of remembrance—a day in which we think of everything we have ever loved.

~ AUGUSTA E. RUNDEL

Yuletide
Around the Globe

Australia

Since the holiday comes in the middle of summer with temperatures reaching 100 degrees Fahrenheit on Christmas Day, beach time and outdoor barbecues are common. Traditional Christmas Day celebrations include family gatherings, exchanging gifts, and either a hot meal with ham, turkey, pork, seafood, or barbecues.

Central America

A manger scene is the primary decoration in most southern European, Central American, and South American nations. St. Francis of Assisi created the first living nativity in 1224 to help explain the birth of Jesus to his followers.

England

"Happy Christmas!" An Englishman named John Calcott Horsley helped to popularize the tradition of sending Christmas greeting cards when he began producing small cards featuring festive scenes and a pre-written holiday greeting in the late 1830s. Newly efficient post offices in England and the United States made the cards nearly overnight sensations. At about the same time, similar cards were being made by R.H. Pease, the first American card maker, in Albany, New York, and Louis Prang, a German who immigrated to America in 1850.

FRANCE

"Joyeux Noël!" In France, Christmas is called Noel, from the French phrase "les bonnes nouvelles," which means "the good news" and refers to the gospel. In southern France, some people burn a log in their homes from Christmas Eve until New Year's Day. This stems from an ancient tradition in which farmers would use part of the log to ensure good luck for the next year's harvest.

GERMANY

"Fröhliche Weihnachten!" Decorating evergreen trees had always been a part of the German winter solstice tradition. The first "Christmas trees" explicitly decorated and named after the Christian holiday, appeared in Strasbourg, in Alsace in the beginning of the 17th century. After 1750, Christmas trees began showing up in other parts of Germany, and even more so after 1771, when Johann Wolfgang von Goethe visited Strasbourg and promptly included a Christmas tree in his novel, *The Suffering of Young Werther.* In the 1820s, the first German immigrants decorated Christmas trees in Pennsylvania. After Germany's Prince Albert married Queen Victoria, he introduced the Christmas tree tradition to England. In 1848, the first American newspaper carried a picture of a Christmas tree and the custom spread to nearly every home in just a few years.

GREECE

"Kala Christouyenna!" Many people believe in kallikantzeri, goblins that appear to cause mischief during the twelve days of Christmas. Gifts are usually exchanged on January 1, which is St. Basil's Day.

MEXICO

"Feliz Navidad!" In 1828, the American minister to Mexico, Joel R. Poinsett, brought a red-and-green plant from Mexico to America. As its coloring seemed perfect for the new holiday, the plants, which were named poinsettias, began appearing in greenhouses as early as 1830. In 1870, New York stores began to sell them at Christmas. By 1900, they were a universal symbol of the holiday.

In Mexico, paper mache sculptures called Piñatas are filled with candy and coins and hung from the ceiling. Children then take turns hitting the Piñata until it breaks, sending a shower of treats toward the floor. Children race to gather as much of the loot as they can.

NORWAY

"Gledelig Jul!" Norway is the birthplace of the Yule log. The ancient Norse used the Yule log in their celebration of the return of the sun at winter solstice. "Yule" came from the Norse word *hweol*, meaning wheel. The Norse believed that the sun was a great wheel of fire that rolled toward and then away from the earth. Ever wonder why the family fireplace is such a central part of the typical Christmas scene? This tradition dates back to the Norse Yule log. It is probably also responsible for the popularity of log-shaped cheese, cakes, and desserts during the holidays.

UKRAINE

"Srozhdestvom Kristovym!" Ukrainians prepare a traditional twelve-course meal. A family's youngest child watches through the window for the evening star to appear, a signal that the feast can begin.

~ JACI RAE
"The Christmas Expert!" and author of Collista's Search for the True Meaning of Christmas!

A thrill flowed through me, while I continued to soak in the pleasures and the atmosphere of my first Christmas in the lush and beautiful island of Jamaica.

~ NORMA CHEW
Retired nurse, freelance writer, poet

A person consists of his faith.
Whatever is his faith, even so is he.

~ INDIAN PROVERB

If there is light in the soul, there will be beauty in the person.
If there is beauty in the person, there will be harmony in the house.
If there is harmony in the house, there will be order in the nation.
If there is order in the nation, there will be peace in the world.

~ CHINESE PROVERB

One kind word can warm three winter months.

~ JAPANESE PROVERB

BALLOONS!

"Red ones, blue ones, white ones, yellow ones.
Any color, get your balloons, two for a dollar."
The voices seem to be coming from everywhere.
The streets filled with kids moving along with moms,
    dads, grandmas, and grandpas.
Even dogs moved in and out of the crowded sidewalks.
Vendors sold their Christmas wares.
Toys, dolls, beautiful paper Christmas hats, and the sorts.
I was overcome with the feeling of festivity.
Small radios blaring.
Reggae music. Rock and roll and Christmas carols
The soothing sound of "White Christmas" caught my ear.
Stopping in my tracks, I listened, became home sick for my cold,
    far away village in Ontario, Canada.
Missing the white, fluffy snow, the fireplace, family, and friends.
Scratching my head I thought, what is a traveling reporter to do?
Suddenly I bought two dozen balloons and started handing them
    out to the kids.

~ NORMA CHEW
Retired nurse, freelance writer, poet

CHRISTMAS IN SWEDEN

*A*Christmas has not gone by when my thoughts didn't go back to one of my early childhood Christmas memories in Sweden, a memory that never seems to go away—instead it now plays a more important part of my life, not only as a Christmas memory but also as a time in history and what this world once used to look like.

I was staying with grandmother in her beautiful but very old and drafty country mansion in the wondrous wilderness of west Sweden. In those days, winters were cold with a very thick layer of snow, the air was clean and clear, and with the red-painted farm houses and snow-covered pine trees around the countryside, the sight was a picture out of a Swedish fairytale.

It was early morning Christmas Day, still pitch dark outside, and it would remain dark for many more hours . . . I was going to church for Jul Otta, Christmas morning service, with my Uncle Alexander, a rather eccentric bachelor who was a known playboy in Paris and on the French Riviera but now had chosen to be back in the stillness of the Swedish forests for the holidays. Why he now wanted to follow the Swedish tradition to go to church on Christmas morning could not have been to satisfy any of his own spiritual or religious needs, but rather an effort to create a special memory for both of us. At least this is how I look at it today.

We had many old sleighs out in the barn, and one of them had now been polished and prepared for our sleigh ride to our parish church located in the next village about eight kilometers away. Grandmother didn't go with us. Maybe she considered the sleigh ride a bit too cold and uncomfortable for her taste, but I was thrilled to be covered in furs and blankets.

(continued)

CHRISTMAS IN SWEDEN (CONTINUED)

I took off with Uncle Alex by my side and with one of our grooms handling the horse. Thinking back, I can still almost smell the cold winter air, mixed with the heat from the trotting horse and the smoke from the burning torch placed on one side of the sleigh. Most of all, I can still hear the sound of the jingle bells ringing through the cold and dark air.

I had been told how each big house had their own jingle bell tone. This way others could clearly distinguish from far away who was coming close.

"Look," I suddenly heard my uncle say as he pointed to the sky. "Do you see the Northern Light . . . ?"

And as I looked up from under my warm furs I saw the sky open to waves of light above us. They looked almost like big white drapes swinging in the wind. What a powerful sight. It felt like looking into the heavens. And in my little child mind I was wondering what it would feel like flying up there right into the shiny heavens.

" . . . When it's very quiet around you, you can hear the Northern Light sing," uncle continued, "It is like no other sound you have ever heard."

When we finally came to church there were torches everywhere to welcome us and to show us our way to the church entrance through the snowdrifts. The dark wooden church, which dated back to around the year 1300, stood in sharp contrast to the snow and glimmering lights. I already knew its history representing many different eras of power and wealth, or hunger and poverty and not to forget the plague of the Middle Ages, when almost all inhabitants of the area were killed by this terrible disease and now were buried there.

(continued)

CHRISTMAS IN SWEDEN (CONTINUED)

Grandmother, in her fashion, had informed me that our family has had its own pew in the church for hundreds of years and that these seats were the place where we were supposed to sit. She had also told me that I had to behave well because everyone would know who I was and it would make her look not so good if I didn't behave my very best.

As soon as we had left the sleigh and entered the church, all the horses would be covered with blankets over their backs and led to their own special stables, where they were given their buckets of Christmas grains, always with a pat on their necks. This was all an important part of local Christmas tradition since horses were regarded as part of the family.

I remember the many candles, the pine wreaths, and the beautiful Christmas hymns, and still today have tears in my eyes when I hear them. But I also remember how cold my feet were and the chill coming from the floor, because the old church was badly insulated from the frozen ground underneath it.

Once back home at the mansion, everyone in the household gathered in the beautifully decorated kitchen for Christmas breakfast. In our family we usually served hot chocolate and whipped cream with Christmas bakery, particularly the traditional sweet Christmas saffron bread, lussekatter, and ginger snaps. And for the grown ups, possibly a glass of glögg, the traditional Swedish Christmas drink, a very potent but quite delicious hot drink made out of red wine, brewed with many spices, and in the end with an additional shot of vodka or Swedish aquavit. I think glögg was created to forget the cold Swedish weather, because it really has that effect on you.

(continued)

CHRISTMAS IN SWEDEN (CONTINUED)

But Christmas Day is not the big day of celebration in Sweden. Instead the emphasis is on Christmas Eve: The day of togetherness, good food and most of all Tomten, Santa Claus. And lots of presents of course.

We always celebrated Christmas Eve the traditional way with the huge smörgåsbord—an enormous spread of all kinds of foods, like pickled herrings, a variety of hot or cold salmon dishes, meatballs—which would always be what I would like the best, not to forget the big Christmas ham, that we would nibble on for days afterwards for breakfast, lunch, dinner, and midnight snack. The smörgåsbord would usually be enjoyed in the late afternoon on Christmas Eve, always with the addition of a glass of hot steaming glögg.

According to tradition on Christmas Eve evening you are meant to handle yet one more late dinner—the traditional Lutfisk. In my personal opinion, this is the most incredibly uninteresting white fish dish in the world. I believe in my own personal way that Lutfisk must be a relic from those times when there was absolutely no food to be found and someone found some old dried codfish hanging around in a barn. To turn it into food, it was then soaked in lye for three days, but to then make it eatable, it had to be rinsed and soaked in water for three or four more days before it could be cooked. People needed something to eat for the holidays and this was it.

As dessert after this completely colorless white fish dish, comes yet one more equally colorless dish: Rice Porridge. To this the cook has added just ONE almond for the whole household. If you were the lucky one to find the almond in your portion, it would bring you great luck for the coming year.

(continued)

CHRISTMAS IN SWEDEN (CONTINUED)

The Lutfisk tradition has often been left out by many Swedes of today—I think mostly because we all so much enjoy the lovely Christmas smörgåsbord, which is quite creative and so very delicious.

Even if you happen to live in a huge country mansion with a large dining room, on Christmas Eve you always eat in the kitchen together with those who mean something to you. Even if you are very sick you should appear for this meal to show the spirit of Christmas. Because at Christmas there are no barriers and no separations. Even the horses at church were shown respect at Christmas. And when Christmas evening is over, you put a dish of cookies and other goodies outside the kitchen door for the gnomes and good spirits of the house as a thank-you for the year that was, as a sign of togetherness in this life we call ours, because this is what the holidays are all about, no matter who and where you are.

~ HELENA STEINER-HORNSTEYN
Speaker, author, www.speakingtoyourheart.com

CREDO AT CHRISTMAS

At Christmas time I believe in the things that children do.

I believe with English children that holly placed in windows will protect our homes from evil.

I believe with Swiss children that the touch of Edelweiss will charm a person with love.

I believe with Italian children that La Befana is not an ugly doll but a good fairy who will gladden the heart of all.

I believe with Greek children that coins concealed in freshly baked loaves of bread will bring good luck to anyone who finds them.

I believe with German children that the sight of a Christmas tree will lessen hostility among adults.

I believe with French children that lentils soaked and planted in a bowl will rekindle life in people who have lost hope.

I believe with Dutch children that the Horse Sleipner will fly through the sky and fill the earth with joy.

I believe with Swedish children that Jultomte will come and deliver gifts to the poor as well as to the rich.

I believe with Finnish children that parties held on St. Stephen's Day will erase sorrow.

I believe with Danish children that the music of a band playing from a church tower will strengthen humankind.

I believe with Bulgarian children that sparks from a Christmas log will create warmth in human souls.

I believe with American children that the sending of Christmas cards will build friendships.

I believe with all children that there will be peace on earth.

~ DANIELLE ROSELLE

HAITIAN CHRISTMAS

I was raised by my paternal grandmother in Port-au-Prince, Haiti. Christmas Eve would be spent quietly at home waiting to go to midnight mass to celebrate the birth of Jesus.

On the rare occasion that I was allowed to spend my Christmas holiday with my mother, it was a different story. She lived a few miles away with my stepfather Edner, my little sister Elsie, and my little brother Lesly in a little town called Bizoton. It was not unusual to have a Christmas Eve party where roasted goat with gravy full of hot pepper was served with rice and beans, fried green plantain, and a green salad. There was also lots of rum, clairin, and soft drinks.

We would then go to the midnight mass while the party continued. Some would stay all night at the party, while others went home to sleep. At around eight the next morning, they gathered together again to eat the seasoned goat "bouillon."

But while the adults would be having a good time at the party, I sat in the front yard with the children from the neighborhood and played Tire Conte, a guessing game. We gathered around and sat in a circle.

"Tim tim, or cric," someone would say.

"Bois cheche" or "crac" one of us would answer.

"Tou rond, sans fond"? What is all round without a bottom?

"Bague," a ring was the proper answer.

"Tim tim"

"Bois cheche"

"Habille sans soti?" What is well dressed but stays home?

"Kabann," the bed.

"Tim tim"

(continued)

HAITIAN CHRISTMAS (CONTINUED)

"Bois cheche"

"Main'm la pran mwen?" Here I am take me.

"Lombraj," your shadow.

There was another riddle whose answer was "Lombrage":

"Kon'm mache li mache tou." When I move, it moves too.

"Tim tim."

"Bois cheche."

"Koto koto co'ou nan Guinin tande?" Big noise, heard all the way to Guinea.

"Lorage," the thunder.

Everyone would try to outsmart the others, even though we all knew the answers. When one of us came up with a new riddle, it was booed at first, then accepted.

Afterward, one of us would tell a story, a "conte," mostly about "Bouqui and Malice." Bouqui was slightly retarded and Malice was very smart. There were hundreds of short stories about those two guys going around the small towns of Haiti. Malice was always outsmarting Bouqui, either trying to sell him as a cheap laborer or making him responsible for some of his own wrongdoing. Malice was always right, Bouqui always wrong. Every one of us wanted to be as smart and mischievous as Malice.

But the story I liked the most was the one about the little orange tree. It was about a beautiful young daughter living with a very bad stepmother. One day, being very hungry, the daughter ate an orange that looked very appetizing sitting on the dining room table.

(continued)

HAITIAN CHRISTMAS (CONTINUED)

When the stepmother found out, she told the girl that she would be killed if she did not replace the orange. The little girl ran to the backyard dump and retrieved the seeds of the orange. She then planted them and sat down next to the bumps formed by the earth covering the seeds. She then started singing with the most beautiful voice, asking the seed to germinate. It did. Then she asked it to grow into a beautiful orange tree, and it did. She asked it to bear fruit, and it did. The stepmother was surprised to see this beautiful, fruit-bearing tree in her backyard.

"That's okay," said the little girl, "you can go and pick some." When the wicked stepmother tried to get an orange, "Quick, orange tree," said the little girl, "grow and grow." The tree grew until it reached the sky and went even further, until the top disappeared along with the wicked stepmother.

When the "raconteur," or storyteller, talked, everyone listened quietly, even though we already knew the story. We told stories about kings and queens, the poor and the rich. Sometimes we all would sing together. When we did not feel like telling stories we made a "ronde," all of us in a circle holding hands, while running to the left as fast as we could. We sang French or Creole songs we had learned at school and teach them to each other.

Oh the wonderful memories and innocence of childhood!

~ CAROLLE JEAN-MURAT, MD
Speaker, author, www.drcarolle.com

MISA DE GALLO

*F*or me, there is nothing like spending Christmas season in the Philippines.

What I remember most is that we focused on the spiritual aspect of the season. Having been under Spanish rule for 400 years, the Philippines is the only Asian country that is predominantly Catholic and the church tradition permeates the holiday season. I remember being awakened by my mother to go to church and attend an early morning mass that started at 4:00 A.M. called "Misa de Gallo" (English translation—Mass of the Rooster). This mass is held for nine days before Christmas, December 16-24 in preparation for the birth of Jesus Christ.

It was tough for a little girl to wake up at such an early hour, but once we got to the church, heard the Christmas carols and completed the service, the festive atmosphere around the church made up for the early morning wake-up call. We enjoyed hot local pastries and chocolate, that tasted so good in the cold morning.

I grew up believing in Santa Claus. I think that this was a tradition left by influence of the United States. I remember that I found out who the real Santa Claus was at age seven and pretended that I still believed in him so that I could get double presents. I think I was ten when my mother told me that I was too old to believe in Santa Claus. I guess at that age, I could not pretend anymore.

(continued)

MISA DE GALLO (CONTINUED)

Although I only have one sister, my home was always full of children. I was blessed with cousins who loved to spend holidays in our house, especially around New Year's Day. We always played games New Year's Eve, waiting for midnight with all the lights in the house turned on (for luck, according to my mother).

My dad always had a huge stack of firecrackers which he lit at the stroke of midnight to greet the New Year literally with a "BANG." That is one thing I miss here in the United States. I'm used to a loud New Year but in my neighborhood, most homes are dark and look like everyone is asleep. However, that does not stop me. I open the windows and yell "Happy New Year" at the stroke of midnight. My kids and grandkids think I am crazy, but once in a while, I will get a "Happy New Year" response from one of my neighbors. All is not lost.

~ CELLY FERAREN ADAMO

POLISH CHRISTMAS

Christmas is a festive holiday in Poland. Many customs, ceremonies, and beliefs center around Christmas Eve, a special day in Polish homes. An important element contributing to its dignified atmosphere are the Christmas decorations, notably a beautifully adorned Christmas tree.

Christmas Eve is believed to affect the entire New Year. For this reason, it had to be spent in harmony and peace with everyone showing kindness to one another.

Today it is still devoted to long preparations for Christmas Eve dinner. All the work has to be done before dusk. Then the whole family sits down to dine together, in the most important event of that day.

Traditionally, Christmas Eve dinner begins when the first star appears in the sky. First, there is a prayer, sometimes with a reading from scripture about Jesus' birth. Then the family wishes one another all the best for the New Year and, as a sign of reconciliation, love, friendship, and peace, share oplatek, Christmas wafers, that symbolize holy bread.

The dinner consist only of meatless dishes. Traditionally, there should be twelve courses, reflecting the number of months in the year. After Christmas dinner, many people end the day by attending the midnight mass known as "Pasterka."

Today Christmas Eve dinner is sumptuous and diversified. Typical dishes include red barszcz, beetroot soup with mushrooms or uszka (dumplings stuffed with mushrooms), a plain cabbage dish with mushrooms or pierogi with cabbage and mushrooms, sweet dumplings with poppy seeds, pastries, cakes, fruit; nuts, sweets and compote drink made from stewed prunes, dried pears, and apples.

(continued)

POLISH CHRISTMAS (CONTINUED)

The main treat, though is fish. The Polish cuisine is noted for a variety of fish dishes: soups, herring salads, fish with sauce, cream or jelly, fish in aspic, baked, fried, or boiled fish. A traditional Christmas delicacy is carp or pike in gray sauce with vegetables, almonds, raisins, spices, wine, or beer.

A popular event during the period after Christmas is the Jaselka, a nativity play staged by amateurs. In the country, you can still see carolers who go from house to house with a star or nativity crib. Traditionally, they expect to be tipped for the visit; once the payment was in Christmas delicacies, but today these have been largely replaced by small change.

The carolers are often dressed up and improvise scenes that loosely draw upon biblical motifs. Typically, the characters are King Herod, an angel, a devil, death, and sometimes a gypsy and a bear or goat.

~ KRYSTYNA MAZUR
www.krysofeurope.net

BOXING DAY

*T*ypically celebrated on the day after Christmas, it was the day when people would give a present or Christmas box to those who had worked for them throughout the year. This is still done in Britain for postmen and paper-boys—though now the box is usually given before Christmas, not after.

In feudal times, Christmas was a reason for a gathering of extended families. All the serfs would gather their families in the manor of their lord, which made it easier for the lord of the estate to hand out annual stipends to the serfs. After all the Christmas parties, on the 26th of December, the lord of the estate would give practical goods such as cloth, grains, and tools to the serfs who lived on his land. Each family would get a box full of such goods the day after Christmas. Under this explanation, there was nothing voluntary about this transaction; the lord of the manor was obliged to supply these goods. Because of the boxes being given out, the day was called Boxing Day.

In England many years ago, it was common practice for the servants to carry boxes to their employers when they arrived for their day's work on the day after Christmas. Their employers would then put coins in the boxes as special end-of-year gifts. This can be compared with the modern day concept of Christmas bonuses. The servants carried boxes for the coins, hence the name Boxing Day.

Because the staff had to work on such an important day by serving the master of the house and their family, they were given the following day off. As servants were kept away from their own families to work on a traditional religious holiday and were not able to celebrate Christmas dinner, the customary benefit was to "box" up the leftover food from Christmas Day and send it away with the servants and their families. Hence the "boxing" of food became "Boxing Day."

Hanukkah

HANUKKAH

Hanukkah (or Chanukah) is the annual Jewish festival celebrated for eight successive days and nights beginning on the 25th day of Kislev, the third month of the Jewish calendar, corresponding, approximately, to December in the Gregorian calendar. It is also known as the Festival of Lights, Feast of Dedication, and Feast of the Maccabees. Hanukkah commemorates the rededication of the Temple of Jerusalem by Judas Maccabee in 165 BC after the Temple had been profaned by Antiochus IV Epiphanes, King of Syria and overlord of Palestine. In Hebrew, the word "Hanukkah" means "dedication."

Colorful candles burning bright, each lit on eight very special nights.
~ UNKNOWN

May the lights of Hanukkah usher in a better world for all humankind.
~ UNKNOWN

May love and light fill your home and heart at Hanukkah.
~ UNKNOWN

THE MIRACLE OF THE LIGHTS

My favorite holiday was Chanukah. Yes, I loved the presents. Yet even more, I loved watching my grandmother, or my Bubby as we called her, light the candles.

My Bubby Jenny escaped from Russia with her husband during the Bolshevik Revolution. She was fourteen years old. She never again heard from her parents and three sisters.

On Chanukah, after dinner, we would all gather around the menorah. Bubby would light the shammosh and sing the prayer thanking God for allowing us to repeat the miracle of Chanukah by lighting the candles. Then she would light the other candles, one for each night of Chanukah.

While she would light the candles, she would tell us how much she loved celebrating Chanukah with her family in the "ol' country." After lighting the candles, she would stare into the flame for what seemed like ages. Finally, she'd close her eyes, sway to a tune she'd hear in her head, and smile. When she opened her eyes, she'd look at me and say, "My family is well. We danced and sang. My sisters and I braided each other's hair. Come, let me show you." Then, by the light of the candles, Bubby would teach me to sing Russian folk songs while she braided my hair.

I believe that my Bubby saw her family in the flames. Her memories brought her comfort and joy. Laughing, singing, and dancing with them one more time was her Chanukah gift from God. Now, thirty years after her death, when I look into my Chanukah night candles, I see her swaying and hear her sweet voice singing to me.

~ MARCIA REYNOLDS, MA, MED
Speaker, professional coach

HOLIDAY SPIRIT AT HANUKKAH

*W*hen a dear friend asked me about my holiday memories, I automatically scanned my mind's recesses for a Christmas tale. He interrupted my search with a simple query, "What about Hanukkah?"

"I'm thinking Christmas," I confessed, all at once surprised by his assumption—and my own.

"But aren't you Jewish?" His tone was both clear and curious.

Having grown up in a suburb whose population was almost entirely Christian, I knew of only a handful of other Jewish families in a school community of thousands. As it was, my family observed mostly high holy days and attended services infrequently. Still, I knew who I was—the Jewish girl in my neighborhood, class, and circle of friends.

While I enjoyed the suspense my mother created around each night's Hanukkah gift, I dreaded Christmas morning, when I would wake up to miss something that engulfed everyone else. I wasn't upset about gifts, but I knew I was missing something more precious—a connection to others, a sense of belonging. I secretly wondered if Santa was anti-Semitic.

As my friends innocently overstated their Christmas experiences, I learned to downplay Jewish holidays. I didn't know enough about the history and religious significance to educate others, so I figured I'd learn about my friends' celebrations. I also knew that Hanukkah was not a "High" holiday and did not parallel Christmas in terms of religious significance. Every Christmas, I got myself invited to dinners, church services, parties, and even gift extravaganzas with treasured friends.

(continued)

Holiday Spirit at Hanukkah (continued)

I was a witness to the magic of Christmas, from its excesses to its sentiment and intimacy. Yet I was an interloper.

When I married the son of a minister, I delighted in my new access to the holiday, which I expected would be finally "mine" as much as any Jewish holiday. My beloved in-laws welcomed me by including a menorah in their holiday décor. We lit Hanukkah candles together, as the holidays overlapped that year.

As if to continue on a path of integrated traditions, my young children now attend the small, private Quaker school where my husband teaches in another, more diverse suburb. This school community celebrates diversity in every sense and fosters a remarkable spirit of inclusion. Last Hanukkah, I felt that first-hand.

In December, the school invited special guests to attend a weekly Meeting for Worship, where the entire school community gathers to hear and honor the light of God in everyone. Each week, the community learned together about a different winter holiday. On a certain date, I was invited to bring our menorah and join my children in lighting the Hanukkah candles before Meeting for Worship.

As if by instinct, I hesitated. Would my children embrace their Judaism? Would they be comfortable with such a distinct label? Would I?

Hoping to set a good example, I went. Running characteristically late, I rushed to the middle of the meeting room, where benches arranged in a sort of squared circle surrounded a center table. Several parents already stood with their children, setting up menorahs and placing candles gently in their holders. My kids ran toward me, beaming with excitement.

(continued)

Holiday Spirit at Hanukkah (continued)

We set up our symbols and soon all ten menorahs were ready. Students, faculty, parents, and members of the meeting had quietly filled the seats around us.

As we lit our menorahs, I was proud to recall the Hebrew prayer and delighted when my oldest child chimed in. Then we silently parted to find seats. I saw some parents nod a warm greeting, as if to say "nice job." I noticed some children, eyes dancing with reflections from the glow of fire, admiring those who got to demonstrate Hanukkah. My own misty eyes searched for my kids, who sat tall and satisfied, having just shared one of their traditions very publicly with their community of friends.

I was struck by the beauty of the light that radiated from the center of the room and by the connectedness that filled it. I was awed by the sentiment, intimacy, and magic of Hanukkah.

~ SONIA J. STAMM

MIRACLES

*M*y name is Lyndon. Yes, I'm a girl. That has been like my last name for all my life: "Yesimagirl." My parents were proud democratic Texans and thought it would be cool if they named me for a president from Texas, as if that would help me be the first woman president. It was torture as a kid. People would ask to see my scar or tell me to quit holding dogs by the ears, or even to stop the war. But now that so many years have passed, and now that parents are naming girls more masculine names like Hunter, Payton, and Taylor, Lyndon seems almost trendy. These days, I get compliments on it.

But this isn't about my name, it's about a guy I know. If I told you his name, you'd recognize it—he's that famous, but back then he was going by "Screamer." Where he got that nickname is beyond me. He has the softest, sexiest voice you ever heard. I guess it's like the real fat people that get called "Skinny" or the tall guys that go by "Shorty."

Leslie was dating Screamer. He played the drums in a local band. It played Deep Ellum clubs and at Fatso's in Arlington. It wasn't like Leslie is a groupie or anything. She hardly ever went partying. But when she started going with Screamer, we were at most rehearsals and every gig the band got.

She met Screamer at a music store. They were both looking for Jesse Norman's latest release. It was hard for me to tell what Leslie saw in Screamer. Besides the voice, I mean. He was kind of scrawny. And it wasn't like he was a celebrity at the time. We thought the band was great, but it didn't seem like the members were trying to get discovered. They seemed to be happy enough just surviving by entertaining.

(continued)

MIRACLES (CONTINUED)

It was easy to see why Screamer fell for Leslie. She's voluptuous, outgoing, and pretty. Then there's that navel ring. When Screamer found out about that and her tattoo, he was a goner.

But usually Leslie liked accountant-types. So, when she announced she and Screamer were going to date only each other, I was floored.

"How are you going to find that sugar daddy you always wanted if you keep hanging out with dirt-poor, rag-tag guys whose idea of a date is a watered down Coke and 2 million decibels?"

Leslie smiled.

"Screamer has a lot of potential," she said. Little did she know then.

I didn't really care who she dated. At least with Screamer, I didn't have to pay cover charges, and I was starting to think the bass player had pretty eyes.

So Leslie and Screamer were together all summer and through the fall. She counseled drug addicts, sex offenders, and incest victims all day and cheered the band all night.

"Do your ears ever get tired?" I asked her once, "You listen to criminals for eight hours and hard rock the rest of the time."

"But when I talk, everyone listens," she said, "Anyway it's not just the listening part. It's figuring out the message."

I told her I could see the challenge in her work all right.; and in her relationships. Figuring out Screamer's message must take days. When he wasn't playing drums, he was playing the sax.

In December, Leslie was making big plans for the first night of Hanukkah. Screamer wasn't Jewish, so it was supposed to be this meaningful, sharing-the-culture experience.

(continued)

MIRACLES (CONTINUED)

She decorated our apartment, polished the silver menorah, made potato pancakes, and even dug out the dreidel. She invited the bass player for my date and Screamer was bringing his specialty, vegetarian chili. We were both looking forward to having a date that wasn't in a club. We were looking forward to conversation without shouting. We were looking forward to real food and real intimacy. For weeks, Screamer had asked the bandleader not to schedule a gig that night.

But you guessed it, a last-minute gig. And the club owner said the line that convinces every band it is OK to break promises. You know the line, the one about the agent who's coming to the club and how this is the band's big chance to get discovered.

I have never seen Leslie so furious. She wouldn't have asked Screamer to make a choice between her and the band. But I didn't think she would ever speak to him again. I offered to stay and celebrate Hanukkah with her, but she insisted she wanted to be alone. So, since the bass player invited me to the club, I went.

I didn't expect Leslie to show up, and I couldn't tell by the look on Screamer's face whether he was disappointed. Maybe I was too busy gazing into the bass player's eyes.

So when the lead singer stopped midway through the second set and said the band had an announcement, I was surprised.

Screamer walked forward with a contraption made out of drumsticks and guitar strings. In all the times I had seen the band, Screamer had never approached the microphone. In his whispery, throaty voice, he said, "There's a lot of talk this time of year about the commercialism. Often we all forget that the season is more about a gift of a life than a guy in a red suit."

(continued)

Miracles (continued)

"But before there was Christmas, there was another special time," Screamer continued. "Hanukkah gets compared to Christmas because they both happen in this season and they both involve gift-giving."

At this point, my jaw was probably on the floor. Screamer giving a speech. And a semi-religious speech in a club at that. And what was funny, everyone was listening.

He went on, "The better comparison is that both of these celebrations are about miracles. Christmas is a miracle of a baby born to a virgin and Hanukkah is a miracle of life, too. Life that was sustained because a very small amount of oil lasted. Both holidays are about light, too. Christmas is symbolized with a special star, a light in the east that led wise men to the baby. And Hanukkah is also symbolized with lights, in fact, it's called the 'festival of lights.' Tonight is the first night to light a candle in the celebration of Hanukkah this year. To mark this special time, I'd like to ask my girlfriend Leslie to come up and light the candle."

I hadn't seen Leslie walk in. But she was there and she came up to the stage, her eyes shiny with tears. She wasn't the only one good at listening, because Screamer had definitely gotten this message. She took the white candle from Screamer's hand and set it in the contraption he'd made.

It must've been the season because several miracles occurred that night. I guess the first was that Leslie forgave Screamer and actually showed up at the club. The second was that there really was an agent there. And the third was this . . . after hearing Screamer's voice, the agent signed him to a contract . . . as a singer. I don't think he's ever played the drums since.

(continued)

MIRACLES (CONTINUED)

Screamer has made it, beyond his wildest dreams. You see his picture on kids' T-shirts. Middle-aged ladies talk about him on "Oprah." His recordings go platinum all of the time. His concerts are instant sell-outs.

He asked Leslie to go to Los Angeles with him. She thought about it, even visited him out there a few times. But she didn't feel right about it. She says she wants to remember Screamer as Screamer, not some pop star.

"But he could be that sugar daddy you always wanted. You'd be set for life," I pointed out. She says she's still got sex offenders to help here in Dallas. She says maybe it'll work out some day, when Screamer's ready to quit touring and settle down.

I said, "That would be a miracle." But I wouldn't be surprised. I've seen those happen before.

~ LORRI V. ALLEN
Reporter, speaker on "Good News!"
www.lorri.com

Better to light a candle than to curse the darkness.

~ CHINESE PROVERB

HANUKKAH

Just as a candle cannot burn without fire, men cannot live
without a spiritual life.

~ BUDDHA

Eight days the light continued on its own,
A miracle, they say, but not more so,
Than ordinary lives of flesh and bone,
Consuming wicks burned ashen long ago.

~ NICHOLAS GORDON

A fuel-less flame is nothing but a wraith,
However wrought, if unsustained by passion.

~ NICHOLAS GORDON
"How Long Can We Remember an Event"

To me every hour of the light and dark is a miracle,
Every cubic inch of space is a miracle.

~ WALT WHITMAN, LEAVES OF GRASS

OUR HANUKKAH CELEBRATION

*W*hen our three sons were young, we celebrated Hanukkah in full style, as much as is possible within the context of a mixed marriage, and without the example of a Jewish mother-in-law who in her quest to be modern in the U.S., did up "Christmas" instead, without a tree, with a huge Jewish style brunch and gifts that were never wrapped in Christmas paper. So we decided to celebrate both holidays.

On the first night of Hanukkah, we read the story of the "Miracle of the Oil" following the victory of the Maccabees in their fight for religious freedom. Each of the boys got to light his own menorah, and we said a blessing. We ate the symbolic foods that commemorated the oil that lasted for eight days and nights. I learned to make latkes, giant luscious potato pancakes, hot off the cast iron skillet and into the mouths of the boys, pausing only for a dunk into applesauce. We ate fresh doughnuts for dessert, which was fun for Norm, who considered himself weaned from them upon marriage. We played Spin the Dreidel, and the boys competed for pennies and who got "Big Red," the lucky dreidel. We bought the chocolate Hanukkah gelt which always looked better than it tasted. We put on tapes of Hanukkah music, got out the big box of toy drums and musical instruments and they marched around the room, happy to make this much noise legally.

Then there were the gifts, one for each of the eight nights, little things, including new socks, wrapped in Hanukkah paper. As time went on, the socks became alternately a source of fun, disappointment, jokes and then, finally, there were none. Our Hanukkah celebration became the one time all year we got latkes, lighting the menorah if we were home, doughnuts, and a little cash gift.

(continued)

OUR HANUKKAH CELEBRATION (CONTINUED)

More years, and the young men began stealing Norm's socks. Even when they were away at college, somehow the new socks at the beginning of the year were never enough. Every now and then, we gave them socks on Hanukkah again, and this seemed a practical matter that was still linked in our minds with the holiday. More jokes. And then there were none. The men were grown and buying their own socks as they started their careers. And then came the e-mail. "Mom, if you're thinking of giving us socks this year for Hanukkah, I could really use some dress socks in dark colors. Thanks."

~ LINDA LOU FERBER

We have focused on the miracle-thing and I think we often overlook the message of Hanukkah. To me, the core of the holiday is the cleaning of the temple . . . . The accomplishment was in restoring the temple to the purpose for which it was built. Now think of the temple as a symbol. Perhaps it represents my life. The world has tried to use me for its own (perhaps good, but none-the-less extrinsic) purposes. But now I can rededicate myself to my own original purpose.

~ RALPH LEVY
"Hanukkah—Another View"

On Hanukkah, the first dark night,
Light yourself a candle bright.
I'll invite you, if you will me invite,
To dance within that gentle light.

~ NICHOLAS GORDON
"On Hanukkah, the First Dark Night"

I ask not for a lighter burden, but for broader shoulders.

~ JEWISH PROVERB

Kindle the taper like the steadfast star
Ablaze on evening's forehead o'er the earth,
And add each night a lustre till afar
An eightfold splendor shine above thy hearth.

~ EMMA LAZARUS
"The Feast of Lights"

Still ours the dance, the feast, the glorious Psalm,
The mystic lights of emblem, and the Word.

~ EMMA LAZARUS
"The Feast of Lights"

Winter Solstice

Now, near the Winter Solstice, it is good to light candles. All the nice meanings of bringing light to the world can be beautiful. But perhaps we are concentrating on lighting the world because we don't know how to light up our own lives.

~ RALPH LEVY
"Hanukkah—Another View"

The miracle, of course, was not that the oil for the sacred light—
in a little cruse—lasted as long as they say;
but that the courage of the Maccabees lasted to this day:
let that nourish my flickering spirit.

~ CHARLES REZNIKOFF
"Meditations on the Fall and Winter Holidays"

By all means, then, let us have psalms and days of dedication anew to the old causes.

~ CHARLES REZNIKOFF
"Meditations on the Fall and Winter Holidays"

Even our misfortunes are a part of our belongings.

~ ANTOINE DE SAINT-EXUPÉRY
Night Flight, 1931, translated from French by Stuart Gilbert

MAGIC OF A WINTER NIGHT

Winter nights are magical,
Refreshing, stimulating,
Chill in the air, dark everywhere,
Bracing and invigorating.

In the early evening,
When the sunlight disappears,
Just twilight for an instant,
And then the night is here.

The black descends so rapidly,
Engulfing everything in sight,
A transformation happening,
New visions in the night.

The darkness separates the people
But each person finds his space,
One cannot see the other,
Though each man has claimed a place.

And there alone inside one's space,
Is when the magic starts,
A touch of softness on one's cheek,
A quickened pulse within one's heart.

(continued)

(CONTINUED)

Look! Look! A snowflake falls,
Then another . . . and . . . another,
Until the sky is filled with them,
And the ground is quickly covered.

The first snowfall of winter,
A miracle, it seems,
Nothing there is quite like it,
In all of heaven's schemes.

Oh, wrap your scarf more snugly,
But keep your face uplifted,
Do not miss a single drop,
With which you have been gifted.

The whipped-cream of your evening,
The frosting on your cake,
Oh what a treat this is,
Each sweetly falling flake.

The wizardry of winter,
The magic of the night,
Our Master waved his hand,
And turned the blackness into white.

~ VIRGINIA (GINNY) ELLIS
© December 2002
www.poetrybyginny.com

WINTER SOLSTICE

*W*inter Solstice is the time when the "sun stands still," the shortest day of the year. In the Northern Hemisphere, days become shorter from June 21 on, until around December 21st, when the sun seems to rise and set in the same place for a while. Then slowly the sun begins its journey toward the south again, and the days grow longer until the peak of sunlight at the Summer Solstice.

The longest night of the year bears within itself the promise of the return of the light, the "rebirth" of the sun. Thus, the Winter Solstice is a time to celebrate the darkness of the womb from which creation arises. We honor the cycles of life, death, and rebirth, the dark night of the soul and the rebirth of new hope and vision. When we move deeper into the darkness instead of avoiding it, we find the gifts the darkness holds. To some, that may mean moving into the shadow aspect of self. What needs to be released, to be brought into the light of our awareness? Even in our darkest moments we can find the seeds of growth and healing within.

The darkness of the long winter nights that culminate in the Winter Solstice is also a time to honor and celebrate the world of the unseen, of dreams, and of intuition. When we cannot see with our physical eyes, we learn to trust the inner vision, the power of insight and inner knowingness. The journey into the darkness prepares the way for celebration: in gratitude we rejoice in the return of the light, the promise of the sun/son lighting our path, the promise of new beginnings.

(continued)

WINTER SOLSTICE (CONTINUED)

A Winter Solstice Meditation

Begin by taking a deep breath in and then exhaling slowly.

Relax as you release the breath.

With each breath you take, you move deeper into the silent space
within, into your inner world.

Imagine yourself now walking through a desert landscape at night.

The moon is not visible to light your path, and at first your steps are
unsure and tentative. The more you attune yourself to the silent
world around you, the more your senses begin to perceive details
along your path.

The desert air is clear and cold, fragrant with the aroma of sage.

Now you move with confidence, you can "see" with your inner eyes.

You are comfortable with the darkness that reveals its gifts:

You can hear sounds of life around you—what do you hear?

You see things you have not seen before—what do you see?

You trust your inner senses, your intuition guides you on your path.

Answers reveal themselves as you surrender to the power of the unseen.

You feel safe and protected.

A warm feeling starts to bubble up in your solar plexus.

The warmth spreads to your arms and legs, to your whole body.

A pleasant tingling sensation accompanies the warm glow that now
seems to emanate from your body, creating a field of pleasant
vibrating energy throughout and around you. The source of light
and warmth is within, always accessible, your internal sun.

You are equally comfortable with the dark as with the light.

You are balanced, in harmony with Mother Earth and Father Sky.

(continued)

WINTER SOLSTICE (CONTINUED)

As you turn your eyes toward the night sky above you, a blanket of
   brilliant stars illuminate the sky.
Gratitude washes over you as you open your heart to the beauty
   of this sacred time and space.
A granite boulder offers a place to rest and relax.
Hours seem like minutes, a sense of timelessness prevails.

Yet, almost imperceptibly at first, you notice a change on the horizon.
The light of the stars begins to fade, and toward the east, the first light
   of dawn colors the sky with shades of purple, pink, and orange.
Slowly the landscape around you reveals a new face of beauty and
   harmony.
Soon the radiant disk of the sun appears and bathes the desert in its
   warm glow.
You are reborn to this new day, and you greet it with joy and
   gratitude.
You can trust the sacred circles of nature that offer new beginnings.
Bless the return of the light as you have blessed the womb of
   darkness that preceded it.

With your next deep breath begin to bring your awareness back to the
   here and now. Feel yourself grounded, balanced, and in harmony.
When you are ready, you may open your eyes, fully back in the here
   and now, bringing with you the gifts of this sacred journey.
And so it is.
Thank you God.

~ REVEREND UKI MACISAAC, MA
www.ukimacisaac.com

CREED
Send forth light into the world.

How high is the mountain yet to climb?
If we look to the heights we may not begin.
We will be exhausted by the distance,
And not step onto the path.

Focus on the present, don't look back,
Except to say thanks.
Don't look too far down the road,
That panic and overwhelm remove purpose and intention.
Delight in where you are.

Know this is the place,
Keep your eyes here.
Be mindful of your feelings,
Express them or hold them . . . but feel!

Take the time to be grateful, to see beauty,
To smile and to remember.
Grant yourself permission to BE,
Experience your essence; you are beautiful.

(continued)

CREED (CONTINUED)
Draw into yourself what is yours,
Leave the rest outside of you.
Own your "stuff,"
Let others keep their own.

Exercise kindness and compassion,
Demonstrate love daily,
First to yourself,
That you may give love to others.

Draw on the strength of God within you.

Admit when you are at fault,
Forgive freely—yourself and others.
Let the little offenses go without notice,
Honor your truth, boundaries, and commitments.

Accept acknowledgement of your accomplishments
with gratitude and true humility,
Love freely and honorably.
Trust and be trust-worthy,
Know you are created with purpose,
And the ability to fulfill and accomplish your mission.
Set your heart to BE this.

(continued)

CREED (CONTINUED)
Ignite your light,
Step onto your path,
Live from your center,
Take the first step . . . the power of one,
and then pass your light . . .

We are created individually and we are unique.
And when we develop into who we are created to be,
We send forth light into the world,
We become a candle and together we become a flame,
A fiery furnace of brilliant blue light,
That can heal our hearts,
And bring peace upon the solar system of our existence.
A holy place where love is unending and our spirits shine brilliant,
A place where each particle forms perfection, and yet remains formless,
And the flames of the oneness in our spirits dance.

~ KATHY HOLDAWAY © 2001

Ringing in the
New Year

HAPPY NEW YEAR!

Sing to the tune of "You Raise Me Up" by Josh Groban

H ow swiftly time flies like the spin of the Fates
A new year with its hopes and challenges
P lan thoroughly and be
P repared for surprise
Y ou will achieve the *success* you're after

N othing fearing,
E xpect all things possible
W ith commitment

Y earning true
E xcellence
A im for nothing less than the best you can
R ise up and shine, ready for anything!

~ LYRICS AGUNG HALIM, INDONESIA

Another fresh new year is here. . .
Another year to live!
To banish worry, doubt, and fear,
To love and laugh and give!

This bright new year is given me,
To live each day with zest. . .
To daily grow and try to be,
My highest and my best!

I have the opportunity,
Once more to right some wrongs,
To pray for peace, to plant a tree,
And sing more joyful songs!

~ WILLIAM ARTHUR WARD

New Year's resolutions, fresh starts, new beginnings:
Each day, we begin again. Breathe and go forth.

~ CATH DESTEFANO
Speaker, www.humantuneup.com

I do think New Year's resolutions can't technically be expected to begin on New Year's Day, don't you? Dieting on New Year's Day isn't a good idea as you can't eat rationally but really need to be free to consume whatever is necessary, moment by moment, in order to ease your hangover. I think it would be much more sensible if resolutions began generally on January the second.

~ HELEN FIELDING
Bridget Jones's Diary

Glory to God in highest heaven,
Who unto man his son hath given;
While angels sing with tender mirth,
A glad new year to all the earth.

~ MARTIN LUTHER

We will open the book. Its pages are blank. We are going to put words on them ourselves. The book is called *Opportunity* and its first chapter is *New Year's Day*.

~ EDITH LOVEJOY PIERCE

A New Year's resolution is something that goes in one year and out the other.

~ UNKNOWN

Youth is when you're allowed to stay up late on New Year's Eve. Middle age is when you're forced to.

~ BILL VAUGHN

An optimist stays up until midnight to see the New Year in. A pessimist stays up to make sure the old year leaves.

~ BILL VAUGHAN

Cheers to a new year and another chance for us to get it right.

~ OPRAH WINFREY

"Peace on earth" is not just a holiday greeting. Every January 1 the Pope issues a message for the World Day of Peace, reminding us that peace is practical, peace is possible, and it is our calling. Peace is practical because it is foundational; without it, we cannot achieve other aims.

~ MARYANN CUSIMANO LOVE
January 1, 2007, www.americamagazine.org

We should never lose sight of the fact that the soul is on the pathway on an endless and ever-expanding experience, and that only by expansion can it evolve . . . accepting the lessons and experiences of the past, and taking the best from everything, we should press boldly forward, looking for the Truth, and ever ascending higher and higher into the heavens of reality.

~ ERNEST HOLMES

Smarter then he should be, David Brett (age ten), watching the countdown to the ball dropping on TV from Times Square in New York on December 31, 2006, "How can it be a good year if we begin it by "dropping the ball?" "Good question" was my reply. *Outwitted by a ten year old* was my thought.

~ MICHAEL BRUCE

SYMBOLIC FOODS
FOR THE NEW YEAR

*N*ew Year foods are thought to bring luck. Many cultures believe that anything in the shape of a ring is good luck, because it symbolizes "coming full circle," completing a year's cycle. For that reason, the Dutch believe that eating donuts on New Year's Day will bring good fortune.

Many parts of the United States celebrate the New Year by consuming black-eyed peas. These legumes are typically accompanied by either hog jowls or ham. Black-eyed peas and other legumes have been considered good luck in many cultures. The hog, and thus its meat, is considered lucky because it symbolizes prosperity. Cabbage is another "good luck" vegetable that is consumed on New Year's Day by many. Cabbage leaves are also considered a sign of prosperity, being representative of paper currency.

In some regions, rice is a lucky food that is eaten on New Year's Day. Our family eats sauerkraut and beans on New Year's Day and it has been a wonderful tradition we look forward to. It's a good time to share good conversation and good food with friends and family. Another tradition we share with some friends is to take a hike on New Year's Day rather then sitting on our behinds after all that good food from the past weeks. Then we go and eat together! Wishing you the very best in this New Year!

~ ELN ALBERT
Speaker, author, www.elnalbert.com

NEW YEAR'S RESOLUTIONS
WITH STRONG INTENTION

Christmas of 2005 I was feeling depressed. All of my younger siblings were scattered around the country celebrating the holidays with their spouse's families. I, on the other hand, did not have a spouse. I had nowhere to go. I was single and alone, 3,000 miles away from "home."

Being the oldest of five children I always had lots of family around me. But this year was the exception to the rule. As I watched from a distance as my siblings created their own lineages, a friend took pity and invited me to spend the holidays with his relatives. As kind as that was, I found myself feeling even more lonely. As I adjusted to adopting someone else's kin on Christmas Eve, a spark all of a sudden flickered inside of me. I realized that, more than any other goal in my life, I wanted a family.

I had been living in Los Angeles for fourteen years, a town where youth is a top priority. Seasons don't change and neither do the faces of its inhabitants. Despite the heat, it is a city where time appears to be frozen. And yet, it is a fallacy. Time still marches on. I couldn't believe that I was thirty-five. For heaven's sake, I still felt twenty-five! I didn't comprehend that the years were passing until I would visit with my growing nieces and nephews. It is in children's faces that the years fly by.

Sitting by the Christmas tree, surrounded by someone else's family, only served to feed the flame of discontent growing inside of me. I had enough. As fun and exciting as my single life had been, I was ready for the next step. I had done everything I had come to Los Angeles to do, and wanted the next adventure.

(continued)

New Year's Resolutions
with Strong Intention (continued)

I was over not having to be responsible for anything or anyone. I was actually bored with myself. I was ready to commit to a new future. Yes, finally, I was ready to find my husband and get married.

I had toyed with the idea in the past, but never before had I felt such conviction that now was the time. New Year's Eve came and once again, I was saddened to have another holiday pass by with no one to share it with. I sat myself down in the stillness of my empty apartment and wrote out my resolutions for the year.

With conviction and full intent I declared that 2006 was the year that I would meet and marry my soulmate! I wrote out a detailed list of what it was that I wanted to create for my future. I also devised a plan of how I was going to manifest my desires. This affirmation set that little flame ablaze and I was propelled into action.

I started to clear out everything from my past that might be perceived as an obstacle blocking me from being seen by my soulmate. I was determined to be the best that I could be so that I would attract the best man for my greatest self. I had been practicing "The Law of Attraction" for about eight years and I knew that if I wanted to create an extraordinary man than I would have to BE an extraordinary woman.

I knew that "The Law of Attraction" worked because I had created an exceptional life so far. I had all sorts of remarkable experiences in my work and traveling the world, although they had mostly been sole ventures. Now, I knew that it was time to focus my attention on finding my life partner. For I knew he was out there looking for me, just as much as I was looking for him.

(continued)

NEW YEAR'S RESOLUTIONS
WITH STRONG INTENTION (CONTINUED)

After begrudgingly checking out online dating sites a few months earlier, I decided to revisit the Web with a new attitude and responded to three prospects. I told all three that I "didn't do e-mail' and if they'd like to talk they could call me. On January 5th, 2006, he called. It was only five days after I had written my New Year's resolutions. He had just returned home from the holiday celebration of Paramahansa Yogananda's birthday at his church when he received my e-mail. He too had been feeling lonely over the holidays, wondering when I was going to come into his life, and moved himself into action to go out and find me.

He drove up from San Diego for our first date on January 6th. There was an instant connection and recognition. For our second date, he flew up to San Francisco, where I was working for the week, to take me out to dinner. We knew right away it was meant to be.

We were engaged by Easter and married in August. It only took me seven months to accomplish my New Year's goals. We traveled to nine countries together in the year and spent each and every holiday together. The secret to my success was "The Law of Attraction." Now, I am getting ready to start to manifest my next goal . . . a family.

I now know that my holidays will be lonely no more. New Year's resolutions can be very powerful if you hold a strong intention, and next year it is my intention to hear the pitter-patter of little feet running around the tree on Christmas morning.

~ KAREN KRIPALANI
Relationship and life coach, author of The Secret of How To Attract Your Soulmate and Get Married Within a Year, *www.BeautyEverywhere.com*

GIRLS' NIGHT IN

*M*y first husband and I were never big party-goers. We never went out on New Year's Eve. As our daughters got bigger, we started staying up to watch the New Year's Eve shows on TV. I would buy sparkling cider and we'd celebrate with toasts at midnight. I had only done this for a couple of years. It turned into a girls' night when my husband stopped staying up with us.

One year, as the New Year approached, I had not really given it any thought. The girls were about eight and ten. My younger daughter asked if we were ready for New Year's Eve. I asked what she was talking about and she said, "You know, the sparkling cider!" I had no idea we had started a tradition, but apparently we had. I rushed out that afternoon and when the ball dropped at midnight in Times Square, we were ready with our champagne glasses filled to the brim with sparkling cider.

My daughters are grown and married with their own children now, but we still get together for girls' nights with a video, popcorn and yep, sparkling cider!

~ JOAN ENGUITA
www.joanenguita.com

Let us dare to dream of a peace that the world has never known.
~ CORETTA SCOTT KING

If you want a better world, become a better person.
~ LYDIA BOYD
Past International Director, Toastmasters International

Your work is to discover your world and then with all your heart give yourself to it.
~ BUDDHA

Let us challenge one another to govern with passion, to govern with zeal, and to govern with a sense of righteousness—but always mindful that we must govern with respect and reverence for our difference.
~ DAWN CLARK NETSCH

Nonviolence is the supreme law of life.
~ INDIAN PROVERB

The Lord bless thee, and keep thee:
The Lord make his face shine upon thee, and be gracious unto thee:
The Lord lift up his countenance upon thee, and give thee peace.
~ NUMBERS 6:24-26

One little person, giving all of her time to peace, makes news.
Many people, giving some of their time, can make history.

~ PEACE PILGRIM

When you find peace within yourself, you become the kind of person
who can live at peace with others.

~ PEACE PILGRIM

Everybody today seems to be in such a terrible rush, anxious for
greater developments and greater riches and so on, so that children
have very little time for their parents. Parents have very little time
for each other, and in the home begins the disruption of peace of the
world.

~ MOTHER TERESA

Let us not be justices of the peace, but angels of peace.

~ SAINT THERESA OF LISIEU

Peace is the deliberate adjustment of my life to the will of God.

~ UNKNOWN

There is nothing so lovely and enduring in the regions which surround
us, above and below, as the lasting peace of a mind centered in God.

~ YOGA VASISHTHA

NEW YEAR'S RESOLUTIONS

RESOLVED, that for the year _____, I, _____, will _____.

It's that time of year again. Lots of people are making resolutions. But study after study tells us that most New Year's resolutions don't last. Why?

1. The timing is arbitrary, not tied to an immediate concern.
2. People frequently make too many resolutions—and they just add too much more to an already full plate.
3. January, with its "iffy" weather, can often be disruptive to your regular schedule, impeding a strong start. The odds are against success—even with the best of intentions. All of which leads us to failure, frustration, and fragmentation—yes, we fail and end up feeling lousy about ourselves. It doesn't have to be.

In fact, I've started advising people against making New Year's resolutions, and in making too many resolutions, in general.

In case you are interested, the Internet tells us that the tradition of making New Year's resolutions began with the Babylonians, whose most popular resolution was to return borrowed farm equipment.

~ JOHN REDDISH
Speaker, consultant, www.getresults.com

A Prayer for the New Year

*L*iving is about expanding our awareness and understanding the Divine nature of our being. I embrace this new year as a time for great fulfillment for me and everyone I love. I know we are guided and directed by an indwelling perfect intelligence, which is God. And I believe that Presence to be one of love, goodness, peace, and wholeness. I declare this year to be one of harmony, prosperity, health, peace, success, and great joy for all.

Believing in the unity of all life, I realize that the goodness of God is part of all people and that we are one in spirit, each unique in our expression and each important to the whole expression of God in form.

I recognize everyone around me as important in God's world. I see beyond our differences to the spiritual essence of perfection, love and wisdom fully manifested within all of us. Knowing that peace the world over depends on everyone, I open my heart and mind to "let it begin with me."

I know that as I express my spiritual wholeness, my life is filled with the blessings that make each day worth living. And I accept for myself and all people the highest and best experiences of health, prosperity, love, success, and joy all year long. And so it is!

~ UNKNOWN

SHERYL ROUSH

*S*parkle-Tude™ Expert Sheryl Roush presents inspirational programs that rekindle the spirit, raise the bar, and create excitement.

Humorous, creative and authentic, she relates real-life experiences in a positive, lighthearted way that enriches the soul. She playfully engages audiences, offering valuable how-to tips while entertaining with stories, songs and surprises. Audiences "experience" her presentations—with lasting feelings, results, and significance.

Participants throughout Australia, Canada, England, Malaysia, Northern Ireland, Puerto Rico, Singapore, the Arabian Gulf, and the U.S. have awarded her top-ratings for content, interaction and delivery style.

She was only the third woman in the world to earn the elite status of Accredited Speaker as honored by Toastmasters International (now in ninety-three countries) for outstanding platform speaking and professionalism. Sheryl was crowned "Ms. Heart of San Diego" for 2004 and 2005, and "La Reina de Esperanza" 2007 (Queen of Hope) for contributions to the community.

Sheryl has presented on programs alongside celebrities including: Olivia Newton-John, Jane Seymour, Art Linkletter, Thurl Bailey, *Good Morning America's* Joan Lunden, *Men are from Mars* author John Gray, *Chicken Soup for the Soul* co-author Mark Victor Hansen, *One-minute Millionaire's* Robert G. Allen, Howard Putnam, *The Secret's* James Ray, and keynote closed for *Commander in Chief's* Geena Davis.

Have Sheryl present an energizing keynote opening—or wrap-up sensational closing—for your event!

Highly customized workshops, special events and retreat facilitation.

Sparkle Presentations
Sheryl@SparklePresentations.com
www.SparklePresentations.com
Call Toll Free (800) 932-0973 to schedule!

Are low morale, high-stress and poor attitudes affecting your customer service, productivity and teamwork today?

Need to rekindle the spirit on your organization?

Bring in the Sparkle-Tude™ Expert to energize positive trends!

PROGRAMS INCLUDE:

Sparkle-Tude!™ Keeping a Sparkling Attitude Every Day
• Discover 7 Sparkle-Tude™ Boosters for home, work and life
• Learn how to deal with difficult people and challenging situations
• Enjoy 67 ways to stay sane and lighthearted in stressful times

Creating a Positive Work Environment
Tips and ideas to bring positive attitudes, connection and spirit to work. Morale-boosting team communication tactics and cooperation!

Customer Service with Heart
Enhanced interpersonal, communication and sales skills with attitude-boosters to generate authentic and exceptional service.

Heart of A Woman, Heart of a Mother, and Heart of the Holidays *presentations*
Celebrations, traditions, tributes and sensational events

Audiences include:

7-Up
Abbott Laboratories
AT&T
Baptist Memorial Health
   Care Corp.
Bucknell University—
   Small Business Dev.
Central California Women's
   Conferences
ChildStart
Columbus Chamber of
   Commerce Women's Day
County of Los Angeles
Ernst & Young
GlaxoSmithKline
Hong Kong Baptist
   University

IBM
Institute of Real Estate
   Management
Intuit/Turbo Tax
Kaiser Permanente
   Physician Recruiters
Kiddie Academy
Latham & Watkins,
   int'l law firm
Los Angeles Unified
   Schools (120 programs)
McMillin Realty
Mitsubishi
Phillips Morris of Asia,
   Hong Kong
San Diego Zoo
Sharp Healthcare

Sheraton
Singapore Press
Sony
Stampin' Up!
UC-Berkeley
Union Bank
US Census Bureau
Verizon Wireless
Westin Hotels
Women in Business
   Symposium
Women's Council
   of Realtors
Zoological Society
   of San Diego